Dinah Luise Leavitt

Feminist Theatre Groups

McFarland & Company, Inc.,
Publishers
Jefferson, N.C., 1980

Leavitt, Dinah Luise.
  Feminist theatre groups.

  "Directory of American feminist theatre groups": p.
  Bibliography: p.
  Includes index.
  1. Feminist theater—United States.   2. Feminist
theater—Minnesota—Minneapolis.   I. Title.
PN2270. F45L4   792'. 09'093 52042   80-10602
ISBN 0-89950-005-6

───

Library of Congress Cataloging in Publication Data

TABLE OF CONTENTS

INTRODUCTION

Through experiments in radical theatre, feminists in the United States have recently been developing additional ways of affecting social and political change. Although the average life span of such theatres is short, they are nevertheless quickly revitalized or replaced and currently number over ninety. They have a vast and diverse potential audience which crosses ethnic, religious, age, social and political lines.

Feminist art is emerging as a direct consequence of the feminist movement. To describe feminist theatre art merely as by, for and about women would be superficial; and to approach it only as a gender-substitute in the male-dominated tradition would be nonsense. The fact that feminism has widely adopted creative media for political expression justifies a sensitive analysis to determine if a distinct aesthetic is developing. Within such an analysis it would be important and useful to know what the aesthetic is, how it differs from other forms, what are its origins, evolution, current directions and, ultimately, its impact not only on its audience but on mainstream playwrights and theatres.

This study of feminist theatre concerns four groups in Minneapolis, a city of great traditional strengths in theatre. They are the Alive and Trucking Theatre Company, the Lavender Cellar Theatre, the Circle of the Witch Theatre, and the At the Foot of the Mountain Theatre. The four groups consitute a generally representative sample of such groups across the United States; each was willing to contribute information. Since these groups are in the same city, impact from cultural factors related to location has been reduced.

This book deals with several questions concerning feminist theatre groups. For example, what is feminist theatre? What are its beginnings, organization, structure, finances, activities, plays, playwrights, philosophies, objectives, audiences and methods of working? What and where are the feminist theatre groups? Who are the fem-

inist theatre actors? How do feminist theatres compare
with each other and with other political theatres? Which
issues of the women's movement are being presented by
feminist theatres?

Further, in terms of its goals, what effect has feminist theatre had? What has been the political and artistic
success of feminist theatre? What, if anything, is artistically unique about feminist theatre? What has been the
influence of feminist theatre on establishment theatre?

The existing literature on feminist theatre, feminist
art, feminist criticism, feminist playwrights and women in
theatre is still sparse, though general information on the
women's movement is more copious each year. While there
exist scholarly works and reference books on the image of
women in drama, the position of the actress in history and
women managers, playwrights and directors, there has yet
to appear a work specifically on feminist theatre groups.*

Interviews with feminists who are not involved with a
theatre group, such a playwrights Megan Terry, Sally
Ordway, Michelene Wandor, Honor Moore, Myrna Lamb and
Joanna Russ; Guthrie Theatre literary manager Barbara
Field; directors Emily Mann, Sheila Reiser and Sandy
Speeler; and university professors Alice Fix and Leonard
Berkman, significantly extended the range of opinions and
information available to the author on feminist theatre and
women in theatre.

In July 1977, the author visited the four Minneapolis
theatres, obtaining taped interviews with members of each
group. Theatre group rehearsals and performances were
attended; videotapes of past performances were screened;
and scripts from each group were obtained for further
study. The Boulder (Colorado) Feminist Theatre Collective
was founded in May 1975 in order to complement research
on feminist theatre with information acquired through
practical experience.

---

*Two recent works dealing with aspects of feminist aesthet-
ics through sampling feminist drama are Rachel France's
A Century of Plays by American Women (New York: Richards Rosen Press, 1979) and Janet Brown's Feminist Drama: Definition and Critical Analysis (Metuchen,   N.J.:
Scarecrow Press, 1980).

Chapter I

FEMINIST THEATRE IN AMERICA

Why a Feminist Theatre?

Feminist theatre emerged in the United States in the early 1970's as an outgrowth of the radical theatre tradition of the 1960's and through the resurgence of the women's liberation movement.

Theatre history has always evidenced periods of intense growth and development usually reflecting and paralleling social vicissitudes. In America the decade of the 1960's was one such period of great political and social upheaval. The reemergence of the civil rights issues and the war in Southeast Asia were two principal causes for this national self-evaluation, whose far-reaching discussions left few American values unquestioned.

Theatre responded quickly to the social consciousness of the times, and although centered in New York, theatre groups sprang up throughout the country to form what Arthur Sainer calls the radical theatre movement.(1)* One can find historical antecedents for this kind of theatre in the work of Büchner, Ibsen, Strindberg, Chekhov, Stanislavski and Meyerhold.(2) Radical theatre activity was not limited to America; European political theatres have stated similar goals:

> to become more directly involved with life; to place the accent on the process of creation rather than on the final product; to establish a new kind of relationship with the spectator, considered on many levels as potential creators; to insist on the actor's creativity; to rethink the role of the director as well as the role of the playwright....(3)

In twentieth-century America the roots of the radical theatre movement can be found in the social drama of the 1930's, especially the Communist Party theatres and the Federal Theatre Project, whose activities are discussed in Chapter VI.

With a great deal of overlapping in goals and meth-

---

*Chapter notes will be found beginning on page 111.

ods, there appeared two discernible trends in the radical
theatre: the   experimental   and   the   political   theatres.
Several definitions exist for each, but in this book, "experimental theatre" refers to those theatre groups of the
1960's which sought to revolutionize, through the collective
or ensemble creation of new theatrical forms and contents,
an art believed decaying.   Groups such as the Open
Theatre (4), the National Black Theatre (5), the Living
Theatre (6), the Firehouse Theatre (7), and the Performance Group (8) belong in this category.   Today their
works are so well accepted that one wonders how early
critics of their work could have been so negative.(9)
Their ensemble acting techniques and methods of exploration have invaded even the most conservative college
introductory theatre courses, and, indeed, even the high
school and community stages.(10)

     Although much of the work of the experimental the-
atres was political, the second branch of the radical theatre was specifically political in intent and method.
Michael Kirby, editor of The Drama Review, clearly points
out the differences between these two types of radical
theatres in his article, "On Political Theatre."(11)   Political theatre groups would include the San Francisco Mime
Troupe (12), El Teatro Campesino (13), the Radical Arts
Troupe (14), the Burning City (15) and the Bread and
Puppet Theatre.(16)   Didactic and propagandistic, these
groups sought to overcome the alienation of players from
audience and politicize the audience with skits and plays
that dealt with the major forms of oppression.(17)   Often
called guerrilla theatres, they performed in the streets,
parks or anywhere people gathered, using a variety of
techniques including song, dance, mime, puppetry, vaudeville, crankies and commedia.

     Both branches of the Radical Theatre Movement essen-
tially sought to replace a theatre that Peter Brook describes as "the deadly theatre."(18)   They were audacious
and committed, daring to ask:

     Why a theatre at all?   What for?   Why do we
     applaud and what?   Has the stage any real place
     in our lives?   What function can it have?   What
     could it serve?   What could it explore?   What are
     its special properties?(19)

Their motivations stemmed from changes in perception
about human beings and their world, and their history
largely reflects a search for adequate means to express
these changing perceptions.(20)

     While theatre groups of the 1960's were attempting a
renaissance, simultaneously the women's liberation movement was reemerging.   Focusing on art and literature,

feminist energies forced a reevaluation of the relationship between women and art and literature.

First, feminist criticism of both art and literature started with an historical analysis of women artists and writers; it examined the image of women in both, and it posed the question of whether or not there exists a specifically female point of view in the response to art per se, the creation of art and the interpretation or appreciation of art.(21) Kate Millett's Sexual Politics became a standard work in feminist criticism of literature and pointed to the fact that historically art and literature have been dominated by men, created by men, and about men and women from exclusively male points of view.(22) Artist Joelyn Snyder-Ott concurs with Millett:

> Western civilization's culture and arts are "male" dominated and "male" oriented. Women's highest artistic achievements are off the scene, seldom heard, or if heard devalued, and finally viewed, but not observed.(23)

Some critics argue that because of "woman's place" in the arts, it is reasonable to look for a feminist aesthetic in women's art and literature. While there are critics who argue that art is neither male nor female, only art, many postulate that since art has generally been a male prerogative, the woman artist's or writer's experience, being culturally different, may require a different point of view from that established for male art and literature.(24)

Instrumental in formulating aesthetics and in giving a voice to issues concerning women and art and literature are such influential feminist journals as Female Studies, Women's Studies Quarterly, Aphra, Womanart, Womanspace, The Feminist Art Journal, Quest and Signs, all founded to accommodate the new scholarship and criticism of women artists and writers.(25)

Increased awareness of women and art also has come through education. Women's studies programs have burgeoned in the last decade on college and university campuses and some schools offer women's courses within certain academic departments. Such schools as Boston University, American Universty, University of Michigan, California State University, Bard College, State University of New York, Vassar and Smith, offering courses on women and art "which contribute to a change of consciousness in the contemporary art student and to a reevaluation of the role of women in the arts and in the academic community" (26), are representative of a larger phenomenon common to our nation's campuses, large and small, public and private.

Women's research centers such as the Feminist Re-

search Center in Berkeley, California, and the Alverno
College Research Center on Women in Milwaukee, have
aided in the collection and dissemination of information on
women in all fields and served as a professional network
for women. (27)

Finally, feminists have formed organizations to fight
sexism actively and facilitate communication among women in
literature and art.   The Modern Language Association in
1970 established a Commission on the Status of Women and
the National Organization for Women has a Women and the
Arts Task Force. (28) In 1970, a group called Women
Artists in Revolution (WAR) organized to oppose New York
City museums and galleries which discriminated against
women. (29)

While literary and art critics, journals, courses, research centers and organizations were propounding revolution in women's art and literature, a less specific, grassroots effort to eliminate sexism was underway within the
women's movement.   Consciousness-raising sessions, group
discussions which led "to increased awareness of the sexist
nature of society and, thus, to more basic analysis and
criticism" (30), were held everywhere as integral parts of
most feminist activities.   Large numbers of private and
public organizations--caucuses, commissions, unions,
leagues, bureaus, collectives, coalitions, task forces and
centers--were established to help involve all women in the
fight for equal rights for women.   Without the work of
these organizations, the idea of a feminist art or literature
would have been purely academic.

Many women successful in theatre directly credit the
women's movement for increased artistic freedom.   Novelist
and playwright Joanna Russ sees a direct relationship.
"Before the women's movement I wouldn't have dared to do
most of the things I've been writing."(31) Playwright
Megan Terry says, "I'd been wanting to write about Simone
Weil for fifteen years, but the women's movement gave me
the courage to do it."(32)

The development of feminism in theatre, however, was
evidenced later than its counterparts in art and literature.
In 1972, a group of women playwrights, Rosalyn Drexler,
Maria Irene Fornés, Julie Bovasso, Megan Terry, Rochelle
Owens and Adrienne Kennedy, founded the Women's Theatre Council.   Rather than develop a specifically feminist
theatre, the council sought to create a professional theatre
which would develop the talents of women in all areas of
the theatre. (33)

Along similar lines the Westbeth Playwright's Feminist
Collective was founded in 1970 by five playwright feminists
in New York to develop plays about and primarily for

women based on the writers' own experiences as women.
With assistance from grants, the group produced their
works for mixed audiences at a variety of New York theatres.(34)

Recognizing the growing importance of feminist theatre in the United States, the American Theatre Association in 1975 organized the Women's Program to provide an
opportunity for members to exchange information and
participate in projects relating to women's theatre.

The newest women's theatre organization is called
Action for Women in the Theatre (AWT). This activist
group has recently published its first project's findings, A
Study on Employment Discrimination Against Women Playwrights and Directors in Non-Profit Theatres (1978).(35)

For whatever sociological and psychological reasons, it
is significant that momentum in the women's movement and
activity in the radical theatre coincided. The women's
movement clearly identified the nature of women's oppression, pointed to its causes and suggested solutions.
Radical theatre content, exemplified by the black-inspired
theatre's vivid portrayal of racism, dealt with social issues
and human oppression, sometimes specifically with women's
oppression as in the San Francisco Mime Troupe's The
Independent Female, which focused on women's liberation.(36)

In an effort to avoid the problems created by hierarchies in male-dominated organization, feminists sought
collectivity in group structure.(37) Comparatively, radical
theatres were often based on a collective structure, occasionally extending their desire for group interresponsibility
to communal living arrangements as did the Living Theatre.
Even those radical theatres which had artistic directors
were far less hierarchically structured than establishment
theatres.(38)

Collective creation was the principal method used by
radical theatres to develop performance material, as in
Susan Yankowitz's and the Open Theatre's Terminal, the
Peformance Group's Commune and the Living Theatre's
Paradise Now.

While the women's movement was encouraging consciousness raising as a means to develop feminist awareness and to discover the woman's experience, avant-garde
theatres were employing techniques of psychodrama, therapy, improvisation and theatre games aimed at releasing
the actor from socialized response. Emphasis was shifted
from Stanislavskian character building to actor self-
awareness.(39)

Feminist criticism, developed by the women's movement, promoted the idea that women's art would have to be

expressed in new forms. Experimentation with new theatrical forms was a hallmark of the experimental theatres,
which usually rejected naturalism and plot for abstract
forms it felt more accurately reflected its ideas.

Finally, the concurrence of women's liberation and
radical theatre movements permitted women to become more
involved in theatre than traditional theatre had allowed.
Most groups, at least as new groups, had open membership
and a collective structure which permitted the entrance of
more women into theatre and allowed them to express
themselves dramatically. Successful women such as Megan
Terry, Judith Malina, Roberta Sklar and Meredith Monk
provided role models for women clearly absent in establishment theatres. The radical theatre provided production
opportunities for many women playwrights of the 1960's,
who then became examples for feminist playwrights. Megan
Terry comments:

> The plays that Maria Irene Fornés, Rochelle
> Owens, Rosalyn Drexler, Adrienne Kennedy, Julie
> Bovasso and I were writing helped the feminist
> movement. Here were strong women playwrights
> for them to see. We turned on a whole lot of
> women to playwrighting.(40)

Therefore when feminists sought to present their
experience and ideology in theatre, they had a recent
tradition to draw upon. It is not surprising that many of
the first women in feminist theatre were former members of
these radical theatre groups. Playwrights Susan Yankowitz and Megan Terry worked with the Open Theatre as
did director Roberta Sklar of Womanrite; members of the
Pageant Players formed the Painted Woman Ritual Theatre;
playwright Martha Boesing, formerly of the Firehouse
Theatre, helped found At the Foot of the Mountain; Carol
Grosberg of Bread and Puppet started a lesbian-feminist
group; and several members of It's All Right to Be Woman
came from the Pageant Players and the Burning City
Theatre.

While feminist theatres freely borrowed from and were
encouraged by the Radical Theatre Movement, they did not
become a women's branch of that movement. Rather,
groups evolved their own styles and methods to express
female reality and the woman's experience from the woman's
point of view, largely neglected by both radical and establishment theatre. Consciously or unconsciously, they were
laying the foundations for a female or feminist aesthetic.
In addition to the simultaneous occurrences of the radical
theatre movement and the women's liberation movement in
the 1960's, one more factor is important to the emergence
of feminist theatre--the growing awareness of discrimination

against women in every area of theatre. Charles W.
Ferguson in The Male Attitude writes:

> In that grim world of entertainment known as
> the legitimate stage, men write, wright, direct,
> produce, review, and advertise most of what
> appears. Women behave as men want, direct, and
> imagine them to be.
>
> Considering that dramas are wrought by men,
> the male naturally holds the attention of the
> dramatist.(41)

Ironically, discrimination was also present in the alternative theatres. Two women of It's All Right to Be Woman
left such theatres because they felt they were not getting
a chance in the male-dominated structure.(42) Martha
Boesing recalls her experience with the Firehouse Theatre:

> Experimental theatres were usually very male
> oriented. However, I felt very present and very
> much a part of the group. It wasn't until I
> became a feminist that I noticed I wasn't as
> important as I had thought.(43)

Lack of opportunity in mainstream theatre has, however, led many women to start their own theatres. "Sexism in the commercial theatre has paid one positive divi-
dend--the unusual number of women who have become
'initiators and groundbreakers' with companies of their
own."(44)

What Is Feminist Theatre?

Essential to an understanding of feminist theatre are
the meanings of key terms, including feminist and political.
The word feminist is defined by one dictionary as "the
theory of the political, economic, and social equality of the
sexes."(45) One must, however, understand that widely
divergent interpretations have been applied to this term.
Even when used solely to modify the word theatre, the
word enjoys a variety of meanings, associations and expectations. Feminist theatre groups have noted that persons
attending one of their performances for the first time often
are surprised that what they actually experience is not
what they had expected. "If it's feminist theatre, people
expect heavy-handed didactic messages and agitprop skits.
They also expect the artistic level to be low."(46)

To some groups there is a difference between feminism and women's liberation, the former term being used to
describe a political theory designed to revolutionize society, and the latter to refer to equality between the sexes
in the present system. Further, both terms, when tied to

a specific theory, such as socialism or Marxism, attain
added meanings.

According to the dictionary, political means "of or
relating to government, a government, or the conduct of
government."(47) Feminists, however, identify much of
what is social or personal as political. Joanna Russ comments, "The personal is political. Nothing infuriates me
more than attempts to mark off parts of life and say you
may not bring your politics here."(48)

Feminist art has often been criticized by male critics
as being too personal and feminist literature as being too
autobiographical. Nancy Reeves explains:

> The gap between male and female ... is not a
> universal constant, but rather the distance be-
> tween public and private that developed with the
> first industrial revolution.... Today the hemis-
> phere of the public has been assigned to the male
> and the hemisphere of the private to the female.
> Each sex has become a symbol for its territory.
> The conflict between them can be seen as a
> reflection of the longing of each to be part of the
> other's sphere, to link the public with the private
> in our schizoid world, to embrace the whole of
> life.(49)

Judy Chicago comments on the public and private in
the performances done at Womanhouse in Los Angeles:

> When we performed, the audience was usually
> shocked, then fascinated by the fact that we were
> bringing the "private" sphere into the light,
> making the private public, and in so doing,
> taking a large step toward bridging the cultural
> chasm between men and women.... Some men
> responded to our performances by calling them
> "therapy" in an effort to discredit them as
> art.(50)

Male reactions to the plays and art at Womanhouse varied.
Chicago continues:

> For some men, this [experience] was profoundly
> liberating, educational, and revelatory. Never
> before had they had the opportunity to see wom-
> en's lives from women's point of view and to be
> momentarily released from the often burdensome
> sense of responsibility imposed upon them by the
> male role.(51)

Other men in the audience were silent, and Chicago and
her students interpreted this as hostility. Chicago, however, reports that artist Lloyd Hamrol "perceived that
many of the men were so overwhelmed by the experience of
the house and the performances that they didn't know how

to respond. [T]he men in the audience were not so much hostile as unknowing."(52)

An extension of the problem of definitions arises in the discussion of politics in art. Feminists see no art-politics dichotomy, agreeing with the view of most political theatre groups. Playwright Martha Boesing states: "I have no problem combining art and politics because I think one is the other. I don't see them as separate. All art is political."(53) Joanna Russ says:

> Your political beliefs are patterns you perceive in your own experience and in the world around you. These perceptions are obviously crucial to what you write. I don't see how one can keep the two apart. My politics must live with me everywhere because the oppression that they are a response to does the same thing.(54)

Feminist theatre is immensely varied. While feminist artists and groups may agree that all art is political and that the personal belongs within any definition of art, they may not agree on a single definition of feminist or feminism. Preconceptions about what a feminist theatre is are danger-ous to any analysis of the phenomenon. The specific way in which each group or performer defines "feminist" is very important to an understanding of that group's or individual's work. Megan Terry believes that people have a difficult time understanding what feminist theatre is because they are too engrossed in trying to identify the political position. "There isn't one party line in feminism. What people fail to perceive is that everybody is an in-dividual and each theatre company projects a different image."(55)

The word theatre in feminist theatre is less difficult to define, but applies to a wide variety of theatrical activ-ities. Since there is a vast range of form and style em-ployed by different practitioners, it would be incorrect to conceive of feminist theatre as relating to any particular theatrical mode.

It is important to recognize that not all theatres com-posed of women are feminist theatres. Groups such as the Compass Theatre, Kuku Ryku Theatre Laboratory, Little Flags Theatre Collective and the Omaha Magic Theatre, although dominated by women in leadership and member-ship, choose not to identify their theatre as feminist although all members may in fact be feminists.(56)

In an attempt to present a range of definitions of and perceptions about feminist theatre, art critics, visual artists, playwrights and women and men in establishment theatre were consulted. How theatre groups define them-selves is examined in the following chapters on the four Minneapolis theatres.

Inasmuch as theories of art pertain to the performing
art of theatre, feminist artists' and critics' ideas are of
value in identifying feminist theatre. Painter and sculptor
Judy Chicago believes that although female art has the
potential for changing men's attittudes toward women, the
first responsibility of the woman artist is to women and
that feminist art content should come from the woman's own
experience.(57) She further writes:

> Once a woman has challenged the basic values
> that define her, those that tell her what she is
> supposed to be as a woman, she will inevitably
> challenge others as she discovers in her creative
> journey that most of what she has been taught to
> believe about herself is inaccurate and distorted.
> It is with this differing self-perception that the
> woman artist moves into the world and begins to
> define all aspects of experience through her own
> modes of perception, which, at their very base
> differ from society's.(58)

Painter and writer Pat Mainardi similarly sees the feminist artist's duty to the women's movement.

> Feminist art is different from feminine sensibility.
> Feminist art is political propaganda art which like
> all political art should owe its first allegiance to
> the political movement whose ideology it shares.
> Since feminism is a political position (the social,
> economic, and political equality of men and women)
> and feminist art reflects those politics, it [feminist
> art] could even be made by men, although it is
> unlikely that at this point men's politics will be
> up to it....(59)

> The only feminine aesthetic worthy of the name
> is that women artists must be free to explore the
> entire range of art possibilities. We who have
> been labeled, stereotyped, and gerrymandered out
> of the very definition of art must be free to
> define art, not pick up the crumbs from The
> Man's table.(60)

The editor of The Feminist Art Journal, Cindy
Nemser, agrees with Mainardi's recommendation of caution
in labeling feminist art.

> I feel it is essential at this time to leave all
> possibilites and options open to women in the
> arts. A feminist art can only be an art in which
> women are free to bring all their individual ideas,
> attitudes, and concerns to every possible content
> and style. Out of this new freedom of expression
> will come an art with its own distinctive form and
> significance.(61)

However, Nemser advocates a much broader definition of feminist art than does either Chicago or Mainardi.

> If only an art that specifically advocated women's rights was designated as feminist, then only women artists who were putting political activism into their works could be said to be making feminist art. But ... any art that reflects a woman's immediate personal experience has the right to be called feminist art.(62)

Nemser believes that it is wrong to condem women who are working in "male" modes and styles. "We cannot call such work masculine if it is done by women"; Nemser continues:

> In the past we have subjected women to phallic criticism in that women's work was only to be taken seriously if it looked like that done by a man. But if it looked too much like a man's then the woman was accused of denying her feminine nature. It would be tragic for us to fall into this stereotyping again today in our desire to discover and define a feminine or even a feminist art.(63)

Clearly these three women are aware of and concerned about the emergent state of feminist art and the concomitant restrictions of labels. Their disagreement stems from whether or not certain works by women artists should be excluded from the feminist category because of a lack of specific political content.

Chicago's, Mainardi's and Nemser's comments on feminist art relate to feminist theatre. The slowness in formulating feminist aesthetics is seen by playwright Megan Terry as relative to the very nature of theatre itself: "Theatre is the most conservative art because it combines all the other arts, has to accumulate all the discoveries of the other arts, and because you have to work with other people."(64) Terry, like Nemser, is wary of labels. She says, "So many people refuse to listen to artists because they are not saying the party line or reinforcing what people already think."(65) Playwright Martha Boesing's ideas parallel those of Megan Terry.

> By definition we are emerging; we don't know the answer. We can't yet say that feminism is this and the patriarchy is that because we have no models for a matriarchy. However, matriarchy is not just the opposite of patriarchy.... Critics must understand what is being attempted. After all the great women playwrights probably won't come for a couple more generations.... The literal idea of being emergent and questioning needs to be praised so that artists dare take those risks. The experimental male theatre has

Artaud and Beckett and even though they may be
experimenting in new ways, they at least have
these precedents.(66)

Playwrights of feminist drama, speaking from the
point of view of performance or drama, provide yet another
perspective on feminist theatre in their attempts to define
it.   Megan Terry feels the sense of community that theatre
can provide is important to women and sees its exploitation
possibilities as significant.

> One of the things feminist theatre can do is to
> explore the possibilites of what a woman could be.
> We don't know what a woman could be like be-
> cause we've had so many outlines and definitions
> forced on us.   Feminist theatre can deal with this
> because with the techniques in playwriting we
> discovered or rediscovered in the 1960's, one can
> explore and dramatize interior states of being.
> Dramatizing these interior states and showing all
> the possibilities or ways to go can really be done
> in the theatre.   That's important for them to see.
> It can start a chain reaction and more and more
> people will see something they can build upon.(67)

Further, she defines feminist drama as any drama that
gives women confidence, shows themselves to themselves
and helps them begin to analyze.(68)

Minneapolis playwright Martha Boesing, whose views
are considered in detail in Chapter V, has perhaps the
most radical definition of feminist theatre.   She states: "I
have never seen a theatre I could really call feminist; most
are woman-oriented 'male' theatres."(69)   While Boesing believes that what is being called feminist theatre is valid
and important, she believes that feminism is only indirectly
related to the women's liberation movement.

> To me feminism is not a movement to let women
> find their freedom within the existing society.
> By definition feminism is a revolutionary concept;
> it means building a new and different society.
> True feminist theatre perhaps cannot be created
> in this society.   The theatre of this new society,
> a matriarchy which embraces both men and women,
> will be a collective theatre which perfoms ritual-
> istic and participatory events that would indeed
> change people's lives.(70)

Thus Boesing sees two kinds of feminist theatre based
primarily on political orientation: women's theatre within
the patriarchy, and matriarchal theatre.

Playwrights working within a more traditional frame,
for example, Sally Ordway, Joanna Russ, Michelene Wandor,
Myrna Lamb and Honor Moore, speak more about woman's

experience and the woman's point of view in drama.

Sally Ordway, formerly of the Westbeth Playwright's Feminist Collective, says that feminist theatre is "the performance of theatre pieces about women and their struggles seen through the eyes of women writers."(71) Joanna Russ says that "feminist plays and performances would be didactic--feminist--in the way one speaks of the political novel." Citing as an example the film, Alice Doesn't Live Here Anymore, she says it "is feminist not just because it has real women characters, but because the topics are specifically female."(72)

Michelene Wandor, coauthor of Sink Songs: Feminist Plays, views the relationship of feminist drama to that offered in establishment theatre:

> Because of the appalling imbalance in theatre in terms of how women are represented, almost any play that takes a woman's point of view has a feminist element in it. So any play which has its focus in women's experience or the concerns of sexual politics is feminist.(73)

Wandor also recognizes the work opportunites offered women through feminist theatre. "A theatre which seeks to change the status of women theatre workers by hiring women directors and managers, and by producing 'feminist' plays and plays by women would be a feminist theatre."(74)

Myrna Lamb, whose The Mod Donna and Scyklon Z: Plays of Women's Liberation (New York: Pathfinder Press, 1971) was the first specifically feminist drama published in the United States, believes that feminist theatre is that which "permits the depiction of human beings--male and female--without stereotypical assignment of roles, character, and personality."(75) Lamb, who views the idea of feminist aesthetics as confining, thinks that women artists must be allowed to define women according to their own personal vision, experience and perception. While she sees no single correct way to present women in drama, she feels that reaching a final awareness is mandatory for a protagonist in a feminist play. Likewise, the audience should both identify with the situation or characters and come to some new awareness, an occurance Lamb has observed following many performances of her plays. "People have said that the Mod Donna changed their lives. Women have walked away weeping from The Two Party System saying, 'That's my life.' Identification may lead to awareness or denial."(76)

Honor Moore, poet, playwright and editor of The New Women's Theatre, says in the introduction to that anthology:

In the seventies, with the shift in the theatre
away from "absurdism" and back to a kind of
realism, women have begun to write from their
own experience.... The women playwrights of
the seventies are not part of a single movement;
they write in many different styles and come to
the theatre with many different life histories....
All over the country, women are beginning to
create plays, not only from their own lives, but
that dramatize history, bring our foremothers to
life. (77)

Martha Boesing supports the idea of writing for the
theatre from personal experiences, but she attempts to
integrate the personal with her community. She says:

I don't sit down and think up a wiggy thing to
write a play about. I feel responsible for my
circle, which right now is a feminist one. Everyone I see is struggling with personal issues....
I feel responsible to write about it. I'm not
interested in writing Broadway comedies or
dramas. They entertain and that's fine, but my
work feels more seriously connected to change. (78)

Pattie Gillespie, chairperson of the Department of
Theatre at the University of South Carolina, in a paper
presented at the 1977 American Theatre Association convention, points out that theatre is an especially suitable
tool for feminism because it can effectively demonstrate the
inevitable relationship between the individual and the
social, the personal and the public:

Theorists as remote as Aristotle and as recent as
Langer have recognized that theatre is at once
particular and universal, historic and philosophic.
Theatre is, then, at its essence, well suited to
display the intimate connections between the
experiences of a single woman and the political
issues of all women, connections which Campbell
(79) argues effectively are the cornerstone of the
rhetoric of women's liberation. (80)

As a writer and historian, Honor Moore is searching
for the literature of women's theatre whereas theatre
groups such as At the Foot of the Mountain are looking for
"the theatre of women's theatre."(81) The participatory
rituals advocated by such groups are hinted at by Moore
in the closing paragraph of her introduction.

The theatre has never been taken away from the
young male god to whom it has been dedicated
since Greek drama evolved from rituals to Dion-
ysus. Women in the theatre are now attempting a
rededication by writing from their own point of

view, in their own forms. The Dionysian rites had their origins in the earlier rites to Demeter, a woman god. Classical scholar Jane Harrison wrote that art and ritual "spring from the incomplete cycle, from unsatisfied desire, from perception and emotion that have somehow not found immediate outlet in practical action." One goes to the theatre not only to find out what is real, to see a mirror of the world, but with a need for ritual, a desire to feel nurtured by the artist's vision--to be taken in, included, not pushed away.(82)

Moore adds that she and other women have experienced not only identification at feminist plays, but a sense of purgation and replenishment.(83)

Carol Grosberg comments on ritual as exorcism:

The political theatre that is being done in the Women's Movement has brought a political purposefulness together with a creative, intuitive source for that political expression, and what's happening now is that theatre is becoming a sort of exorcism --a recognition through participation in that theatre.(84)

The views thus far presented are wholly female ones because, except for scattered reviews of feminist dramas and productions, men have not publicly discussed feminist theatre. Leonard Berkman, playwright and professor of theatre at Smith College, in a letter to the author, offers one male point of view. Berkman sees a feminist drama as one which takes into account the social ambiance which fosters specific gender roles.

Simply a dramatic perception of that ambiance is already feminist because it is causing the audience to realize that what may seem "natural" to some is in fact not inevitable gender behavior but influenced by choice.

The valuing and communication of women's experience in all types of interaction is a component of Berkman's definition. He notes in the letter, however, that women's experience can be communicated without any feminist consciousness whatsoever.

In particular, women writing about their own lives can often provide material for feminist interpretation that is not inherently feminist itself. Feminist drama values women's lives, whatever the perspective the women (characters in this instance) take toward their own lives; but feminist drama adds to the sheer portrayal of such lives the perception into the social ambiance which

affects how the women are viewing their own
lives.
    A play which simply has challenging roles for women
or a strong female protagonist would not on that basis
alone qualify as a feminist play.
        Feminist drama gives particular attention to the
        lives of women in terms of their mental and phys-
        ical needs, placing these needs at the center of
        the drama rather than giving them importance
        only in relation to the men in these women's
        lives, or to the services the women perform in a
        male-dominated world.
    Berkman, a feminist and a playwright, believes that
because males are capable of perceiving the social ambiance
that confines men and oppresses women, they are capable
of writing feminist drama. This question brings up the
larger one of whether or not anyone can understand the
experience of a person of differing race, religion, nation-
ality or sex. Berkman says in his letter:
        I think we must face the idea of projecting
        another's experience with considerable humility.
        But I do not feel we should throw up our hands
        as though, because the whole of another's exper-
        ience may not be captured or accurate, the at-
        tempt is worthless, research and imagination
        futile.
Berkman adds that attempts by both men and women to
explore the other's experience can promote the cross-sex
understanding essential to social change. (85)
    A summary of these varied observations on feminist
theatre reveals, first, that the phenomenon's current
emergent condition defies labels. While critics and practitioners agree that an aesthetic or a set of criteria for
evaluation is necessary if feminist theatre were to be
recognized as more than a fringe, experimental fad, they
are hesitant to identify one as yet.
    It has been determined that feminist theatre and art
are political and associated with the women's movement.
An understanding of feminist theatre presupposes a knowledge of the political movement which itself allows much
room for various definitions and interpretations which must
be understood in the context used by each group or
performer. Arguments over whether art by women is
feminist or not seem useless in the light of the larger
awareness that since all art is political, all works will be
either feminist or non-feminist regardless of the gender of
the artist.
    The emerging state of both feminism and feminist
theatre engenders the theatre's variety in subject and

style and its visionary but non-prescriptive point of view.
Feminist drama arrives at the universal through the personal; it emanates from the artist's own experience and
values that experience.   Plays that merely focus on women
or provide challenging roles for them are not necessarily
feminist.   The simple inclusion of pro-woman, anti-
chauvinist lines of dialogue within a play does not make it
feminist unless the larger context of the play bears out
the perceptions of those lines.

Feminist theatre is pro-woman, even when presenting
negative images of women, because it explores the possibilities open to them.   Performances, designed to provide a
consciousness-raising experience for the audience, may
speak more to women at this time but also are intended for
and may be created by men.

Feminist theatre is didactic, because it supports a
cause, but its didacticism ranges from overt, simplistic
agitprop to subtle, complex drama.

Although feminist theatre encourages women entering
all areas of theatre art, it is more than just a response to
the lack of opportunity for women in mainstream theatre
due to discrimination.   Some theatres seek to give women
opportunities to work in theatre or to develop skills;
others attempt to discover a specifically feminist theatre
art, but both focus on women's needs and offer alternatives to dominant partiarchal theatre.

Although no two feminist theatres are identical,
certain common characteristics such as collective organization, process-orientation, focus on the woman's experience, community involvement, lack of money and use of
experimental developmental techniques are discernible
among them.   The Minneapolis feminist theatre groups are
generally representative of the feminist theatre phenomenon
in the United States today, and major differences among all
groups relate more to disparities in degree than in kind.

Since feminist theatre is a relatively new genre, it is
difficult to establish distinct categories for theatre groups.
However, whether groups are classified according to political orientation, amount of persuasion in their drama,
degree of professionalism, success in fulfilling goals, their
relationship to establishment theatres or any other criteria,
a study of these Minneapolis groups will show the general
direction American feminist theatre group activity is taking.

The only type of feminist theatre not represented by
these four companies is a feminist theatre which seeks primarily to act as an avenue for women artists into mainstream theatre by providing exposure and work opportunities, as does New York's Interart Theatre.   However,
this kind of feminist theatre is rare and seldom employs a

constant company of performers as do other groups.

Feminist Theatre Groups: Four Pioneers

The first mention of feminist theatre in a recognized theatre journal appeared in June 1972 in The Drama Review. Author Charlotte Rea examined the structures, philosophies and performances of three New York groups, one Los Angeles group and one Canadian group.(86)   Because of isolation and the concomitant poor intergroup communication, the lack of media attention and the ephemeral nature of feminist theatre groups, it is difficult to investigate the first theatres--even to determine which one was the very first.   It is known that the pioneers of feminist theatres include the New Feminist Theatre (1969), It's All Right to Be Woman (1970), the Westbeth Playwright's Feminist Collective (1970) and the Washington Area Feminist Theatre (1972).   Of these four, the Washington Area Feminist Theatre lasted the longest time, continuing into 1978.

The New Feminist Theatre was founded in New York City in a traditional theatrical mode by its leader-director, Anselma dell'Olio, who previously had been unsuccessful in getting feminist material into the repertory of existing political theatres.   Composed of both men and women members, the group sought to:

contribute to the liberation of women from centuries of political, social, economic, and above all, cultural oppression.   By this we mean not just "to give women a chance" in the arts, though necessarily, feminist theatre will be composed mostly of women, but primarily to give a dramatic voice to the new feminist movement.(87)

The group worked in several fashions: creating their own pieces through improvisation as in their Cabaret of Sexual Politics, improvising from written material such as Jules Feiffer's Marriage Manual, and producing scripted dramas including Myrna Lamb's But What Have You Done for Me Lately?.   Performance content was to be feminist, but dell'Olio believed that the theatre's responsibility was to reach as many people as possible with feminist material, not necessarily to seek new forms.   Accordingly, the New Feminist Theatre sought the establishment theatre's audience.   This was in contrast to other groups, including the It's All Right to Be Woman, which relied on support from feminists, sometimes to the extent of excluding men from certain performances.(88)

The primary objective of the It's All Right to Be

Woman Theatre was "to make women feel that the condition of being woman (not individual woman, but collective woman) is all right."(89) The eleven-member, all-woman group was organized into a collective; all decisions and actions were made with collective approval. All performance material was group-created, based on the lives of the actresses and developed by months of work in consciousness raising, movement and acting exercises.(90)

In performance, the group usually presented a sequence of short pieces interspersed with songs and audience involvement. Pieces dealt with lesbianism, rape, the dependency of women on men and dreams. In their dream plays a performer or audience member would relate a dream while the group, who had not heard it previously, acted it out in pantomime. One player assumed the role of the dreamer, and the rest became the characters, props and scenery of the dream. As with any improvisational technique in performance, artistic success was erratic. However, the attempt revealed the psychological exploration the group felt was important in determining just what was the female experience.(91)

The Westbeth Playwright's Feminist Collective grew out of the Westbeth Apartments tenant's association. Eventually playwrights from the association got together with actors to have the opportunity to hear their works-in-progress read and performed. All professional playwrights, the authors, Gwen Gunn, Patricia Horan, Chryse Maile, Sally Ordway, A. Piotrowski, Dolores Walker and Susan Yankowitz, had shows produced at the New York Public Theatre, Cafe La Mama, the Open Theatre, Eugene O'Neill Theatre, Mark Taper Forum and Lincoln Center.(92) Charlotte Rea describes their goals:

> Besides endeavoring to work within the non-authoritarian group structure as an expression of their feminist convictions, the playwrights are also exploring the female consciousness in their scripts, trying to develop serious, three-dimensional roles for women.(93)

Essentially a playwright's workshop, the collective hired actors and directors for performances. Occasionally some of the members acted in other members' plays. Their first show, Rape-In, in 1971, composed of four short plays, Gunn's Across the Street, Ordway's Crabs and There's a Wall Between Us Darling, and Walker's Abide in Darkness, was followed in 1972 by Up!, a revue which dealt with the various roles that women are forced to play in life.(94)

Although organized sometime after the New Feminist Theatre, It's All Right to Be Woman and the Westbeth

Playwright's Feminist Collective, the Washington Area Feminist Theatre (abbreviated to W.A.F.T.) was an important group because of its successful efforts to put feminist theatres and feminist playwrights into contact with one another through its clearinghouse bulletin. Performing primarily scripted works, the collective has produced plays of Myrna Lamb and Megan Terry, new works by Elwil Hughes, Leslie Jacobson, Mary Koisch and Judith Katz, historical plays of Aphra Behn, Lillian Mortimer, Rachel Crothers and Susan Glaspell, and the winning selections from the W.A.F.T. Bicentennial Playwriting Contest.(95) In the spring 1975 W.A.F.T. Newsletter, the collective stated its goal as "to collectively explore, communicate and further feminist ideals through quality theatre."(96)

In addition to performances, W.A.F.T. was very active in an internship program with Antioch College, teaching courses at Mt. Vernon College, offering workshops in theatre, dance, and playwriting and sponsoring other feminist artists in the Washington, D.C., area.(97)

The polarity that exists between the theatrical emphasis of the New Feminist Theatre and the Westbeth Collective and the psychological/sociological emphasis of the It's All Right to Be Woman seems linked to the degree of acceptance by each group of the traditional theatrical framework.

> The groups that are seeking new forms to reach women and are committing themselves to an internal structure expressive of their consciousness, tend to affect the audiences more intensely than the groups whose framework and commitment is to feminist theatre within traditional forms.(98)

Expressing a new awareness through new theatrical forms is not an easily realized goal. Visual artist Judy Chicago has observed an initial overt stage in the work of women student artists as they become connected with feminism. "This art is often an attempt to articulate feelings for which there is, as yet, no developed form language."(99) Initial efforts at feminist theatre seem to parallel the woman visual artist's experience in that, having no feminist tradition, they often revert to the accepted forms of establishment theatre.

In feminist theatre the overt stage is often apparent in dramatic content. Early works are frequently propagandistic and didactic, coming from the women's feelings of outrage and anger at their oppression. However, in groups that endure, an evolution occurs which allows transcendence of this awkward phase. An article about the Westbeth Collective written three years after the formation of the group states:

Oppression is not the primary focus of their work, nor is anger. The Westbeth Collective has progressed far beyond these hackneyed perceptions of incipient feminist consciousness. Their consciousnesses have been raised. Consequently, the group concentrates on building a repertory of plays written by women based on the truths that self-awareness wrought. Anger, they say, has changed our lives, but more importantly, our anger has evolved from desperate bursts of helpless rage into constructive, more specific and lasting responses.(100)

These four first feminist theatres each failed to produce collectively any significant drama, perhaps because of their overtly didactic content and their reliance on forms reminiscent of the brief satirical skits of the political theatres. Some early theatres evolved from this stage to produce more sophisticated and original work. Newly organized feminist theatre groups are prone to this same response and, unfortunately, through their isolation, are often unable to profit from previous groups' experiences.

Even without the benefit of the knowledge and experience of their forerunners, new feminist theatres appeared all over the United States in the 1970's. In 1975, Ms. published the results of a feminist theatre group survey which was admittedly incomplete and selective. Their annotated listing described the activities of 23 theatre groups, six in California, two in Massachusetts, two in Minnesota, ten in New York and one each in Washington, D.C., Rhode Island and Washington state.(101) The W.A.F.T. Clearinghouse Bulletin published in 1975 the names and addresses of 17 feminist theatres, adding to those recognized by Ms. two more Minnesota groups and one theatre each in Washington, D.C., Massachusetts, New York, Georgia and Pennsylvania.(102) Linda Walsh Jenkins, editor of Women in Performing Arts Newsletter, reported in the April 1977 issue the existence of 11 feminist theaters, only three of which had been included in the Ms. and W.A.F.T. surveys. Illinois and Nebraska were added to the list of states with feminist theatres, while New York, Massachusetts, Minnesota and California added more groups.(103) Not included in the selections of the aforementioned lists are groups from Iowa, Colorado, New York, Massachusetts and Pennsylvania which participated in the Wilma Project's "New Theatre Festival, Womanstyle," held in July 1976 in Philadelphia. In its December 1977 issue, devoted to women in the arts, Ms. updated its 1975 survey by listing another 14 feminist theatres.(104) These selective surveys, which have undoubtedly missed some groups, reveal the existence of over fifty groups representing every region of the United States.

Widespread as the phenomenon is, there is a great deal of diversity among groups. The philosophy of each group is expressed differently, but generally they declare a desire to express female reality and the woman's experience, which has been denied in traditional theatre. Their methods vary from the W.A.F.T.'s use of scripts, to the Rhode Island Feminist Theatre's employment of ensemble acting to create plays collectively, to At the Foot of the Mountain's group-playwright collaborations. Other performance types include the Sunshine Company's puppet theatre, the Commonplace Pageant's mime shows, the Co-Respondents' reader's theatre, the Feminist-Socialists Collective's guerrilla theatre, Motion's improvisational theatre and the Open Stage's children's theatre.

Indicative of their commitment to their audiences, most groups hold discussion sessions following performances and offer acting workshops to the public. Groups such as the Co-Respondents, Earth Onion, and Bread and Roses have extensively toured their shows in the United States and Canada, enlarging their audience and their accessibility.

Countless distinctions between feminist theatre groups could be made. Certainly the Co-Respondents' focus on women's history in reader's theatre contrasts with the Rites of Women's abstract woman-rituals. This incredible variety in style and content reinforces the idea that feminist theatre is not a narrowly specific kind of theatre designed for a small public. Its desire to present the "other half of art," woman's experience, if realized, would aid in making "universal," when used to describe art, a veritable description.

Chapter II

THE ALIVE AND TRUCKING THEATRE COMPANY

The now defunct Alive and Trucking Theatre Company was organized in Minneapolis, Minnesota, in May 1971, by Lori Hanson and Ray St. Louis. After seeing the Madison Street Theatre perform the San Francisco Mime Troupe's The Independent Female at a women's conference in Madison, Wisconsin, they gathered together a group in Minneapolis to perform that same play. From the cast of this production a permanent feminist theatre company was formed.(1) The group named itself the Alive and Trucking Theatre (abbreviated as the A & T) to reflect its energy, involvement and forward-moving efforts.(2) Although the company evolved considerably in its five-year history, its initial performance style and group attitude was significantly influenced by the San Francisco Mime Troupe.(3)

Membership, always predominantly female, fluctuated from eight in October 1971 (4) to ten (six women and four men) in 1972 (5), to nine women, six men and three children in 1973.(6) Membership was parttime or fulltime as determined by the individual's degree of involvement in company activities.(7) Recruitment of new members was handled in several ways.

> At first anyone who came and hung around long enough was included. Later we held weekly workshops open to the public, as a way of working with people who were interested in the group. At other times ... we held public auditions.(8)

Theatre training was never a membership requirement, and only two members had formal theatre training.(9) The members, however, did possess skills in gymnastics, mime, dance, music, writing and technical theatre.(10) The membership was consistently composed of white, middle-class women and men, primarily in their twenties, although the group sought members from other races, age groups and economic classes.(11) Member Jan Mandell explains: "If you're trying to reflect society, it's harder to do it if

23

you don't have all the different kinds of people."(12) For
this same reason men were unconditionally admitted to the
group, but this was not true of other feminist groups in
Minneapolis. "We did not discuss becoming an all women's
theatre group because our experience with The Independent Female indicated to us that we could successfully deal
with the issues of feminism in a mixed group."(13)

The A & T was originally housed in a building in
South Minneapolis that was scheduled to be demolished and
was, in fact, replaced by a highrise a year later. This
space was rented for $100 per month and equipped with a
crude, homemade lighting system.(14) After the loss of
its theatre, the group operated out of a bus and later a
van with a portable stage and technical accouterments
that could be set up wherever the group performed.(15)

In organization and structure the A & T was a collective; all decisions were group made and all work was
shared. Collectivity was closely associated with the
group's political position and reflected its rejection of
competitiveness and hierarchies. In order to share skills,
jobs were rotated among members. This practice avoided
job sex-role stereotyping such as the men building the
sets and the women making the costumes.(16) Meri Golden
writes:

> Our collective production process may take more
> time than an individual whipping out a script or
> actors simply learning lines or blocking stage
> movements, but we all feel that the production
> process is a reflection of us as a collective as
> well as a reflection of our audience.(17)

Jan Mandell says that the collective process changed
as the theatre grew.

> We started originally with everybody doing every-
> thing and found it inefficient. This process also
> inhibited the full development of skills we wished
> to share. We learned, however, that everybody
> did not have to be involved in minor decis-
> ions.(18)

Maintaining the collective structure and increasing
efficiency was achieved through the rotation of duties and
through several committees which formed as needs arose.
Production committees for writing, directing and technical
work were set up for each show. Political education
committees, outreach committees and booking committees
operated to fulfill the needs of the group and its audience.(19) Two office staff positions, the only fulltime paid
positions in the company, rotated among members and were
seen as essential to efficient operation.(20)

While the A & T held no official ties with any political

organizations, it had informal affiliations with many, including the New American Movement and, one that some A
& T women helped form, the Twin Cities Women's
Union.(21)   Cooperation with other organizations was
important to the A & T for two reasons.   First, it helped
the group relate better to the communities it served.   For
example, the Northeast Neighborhood Organization, faced
with threats of urban renewal, worked with the group to
produce and perform skits in neighborhoods to help inform
and urge active resistance.(22)   Audience-performer cooperation is used in this same manner by many political
theatres, notably in the United States.   El Teatro Campesino included the United Farm Workers in the creation of
its plays.(23)   In France the Nouvelle Compagnie d'Avignon met with factory workers to create Emballage and with
the citizens of Avignon to produce A becs et a griffes.(24)

Second, the A & T realized the need for a method of
action that political groups could provide.   Meri Golden
states:

> We felt the need to link with organizations because
> once we had raised the audiences' conscious-
> nesses, hopefully they would want to move to
> action and would need a vehicle for that
> action.(25)

Although avoiding specific political advice in its productions, the A & T strongly held the view that presenting
the problem was insufficient and that projecting means for
collective audience action was necessary.(26)

Economic problems, usually present in political theatres, plagued the A & T.   Jan Mandell explains:

> If you're a political theatre you do not want
> money from sources who will manipulate your
> work.   The alternative is open grants which are
> hard to get unless you're established and artistic-
> ally respected.   A & T had not developed to that
> point yet, but there's a Catch 22.   If you're
> going to play for audiences for little money, there
> is little profit and little for lessons or technical
> equipment which would improve your artistic
> quality.   Also if you have a message in your art,
> it gets called propaganda.   Why would the Arts
> Council want to fund propaganda?(27)

However, the group did eventually receive grants from
foundations, including the Wilder Foundation, the Minnesota State Arts Council and the Hennepin County Bicentennial Commission (28), indicating that perhaps those
awarding grants began to acknowledge the artistic merit of
the A & T's work.

The A & T was incorporated as a non-profit organ-

ization, and its members, with the exception of staff
personnel, held jobs outside the theatre. In order to
appeal to a non-affluent audience, admission prices were
kept low, ranging from free to $2.50. Gross earnings
including grant monies were estimated for 1975 at $15,000.
Chief disbursements were for production costs and staff
salaries of $250 per month per worker. All property,
including technical theatre equipment, stage props, sets,
costumes and a van, were collectively owned.(29)

The collective structure of the A & T is the most
important element in understanding its philosophy and
goals. The collective process of creating plays, detailed
below, and the group's organization and life style reflected
its political ideals. Its purpose was to provide "tools and
spirit to both motivate resistance against an unjust system
and build a new, more humane society."(30) Rejecting
most establishment theatre as irrelevant and designed to
lull, muffle and blind, it was dedicated to raising issues
and consciousness through theatrical forms and content
which were clear and straightforward.(31)

Committed to its community, the A & T's play's content frequently was inspired by community problems such
as unemployment, urban renewal, daycare and welfare, as
well as larger issues of racism, capitalism and sexism.(32)
In form, the A & T frequently chose satire, humor and
musical comedy to present its message because these forms
suited its ideas and the members' theatrical competence.(33)
Seeking to create and perform plays from members' own
life experiences as buffered by community input, the theme
of many of their pieces was that "by acting together
people are more likely to effect the changes they want and
ultimately feel strengthened and hopeful about their
lives."(34)

In order to realize its goals, the A & T worked in
rehearsal an average of twenty hours per week, plus time
spent for business meetings, outside theatre courses,
political study sessions, maintenance tasks and criticism/
self-criticism sessions.(35) Working from the idea that the
process was equally as important as the end product, and
that discordance within the group would affect both process and product, the company employed the technique of
criticism/self-criticism to foster group unity and to provide
an outlet for individual's feelings.(36)

Rehearsals employed well-known techniques of improvisation, theatre games and vocal and physical exercises.
Jerzy Grotowski's Towards a Poor Theatre is cited as an
early source of theatre exercises. Frequently one member
took an acting or directing class in order to teach the
other members.(37) Rehearsal techniques naturally varied

with each play and with the stage of development of that creation.

In an article published in <u>Common Ground</u>, Meri Golden outlined the play creation process that the A & T had developed by 1975.

> (1) The idea for the topic of the play ... is based on study and discussion of issues important to us as individuals and community members. Proposals for new play topics, written by one or two people, are based on our discussion with individuals and organizations. Often plays are written out of our own experience.... We use criticism/self-criticism in discussing the merits and drawbacks of each topic.
>
> (2) After the play topic is decided upon, a committee, made up of people who are already skilled and those who want to learn the skills, takes the ideas and develops a political outline and a plot outline. The former clearly points out what we want to demonstrate in each scene.
>
> (3) The collective discusses this outline and we all talk with people in the community for input.
>
> (4) Our acting improvisations begin and we invite people who have worked on the issues involved to help us in rehearsal.
>
> (5) The next step is further improvisations aimed at developing characters. At this time the show is cast.
>
> (6) The plot outline is shaped by our improvs and then broken down into beats.
>
> (7) At this point, following continued improvs, we work on music, songs, dances, etc. A committee then takes the script and develops dialogue.
>
> (8) The dialogue is tried out in rehearsals and modified by our improvs until
>
> (9) [The dialogue] is finally set.
>
> (10) From there we follow more traditional theatre patterns of technical duties (costume, make-up, lights) as well as business tasks including publicity and fundraising.

(11) The play is rehearsed and polished with
community members invited for criticism and is
finally ready to open.

Our plays are constantly in progress as we solicit
community discussion of our performances. It is
this element, including the audience in the creative process (which gives the audience power),
that distinguishes A & T from other theatres.(38)

Explication of two A & T plays, Pig in a Blanket and
Battered Homes and Gardens, toward the end of the chap-
ter, will clarify the company's methods and show trends in
performance, content and style. The major collective
works of the A & T are: Pig in a Blanket; The People
Are a River;   Rats, Bats, Hells, Bells, and Son of Evil
Genius; The Welfare Wizard of Ours; Ally, Ally, All Come
Free; Battered Homes and Gardens; and Clown Wanted.
The troupe also produced Brecht's The Exception and the
Rule, the San Francisco Mime Troupe's The Independent
Female as well as dozens of street and guerrilla theatre
pieces.(39)
Pig in a Blanket was the group's first collectively
written play. In 18 short scenes the play examines the
major forms of sex-role stereotyping and issues of sexual
politics.
The second play, The People Are a River, opened in
summer 1972 and focused on Minneapolis history from the
working person's point of view. The two-hour production
used "dialogue, music, dance, visual effects ... and an
impressive show of slides from the Minnesota Historical
Society" to sum up almost every important struggle of
working people against greedy speculators and capitalists
that ever happened in the state.(40) The episodic plot
was held together by a narrator named the Spirit of the
People. Examining human oppression, the play gave an
equally strong voice to women's oppression, including
forced sterilization of women to control population and
discrimination against married women.
Rats, Bats, Hells, Bells, and Son of Evil Genius was
developed with school children aged eight to 15 in an
alternative school in Minneapolis. Touring schools and
education conferences, the play portrayed a school system
of manipulated students dominated by sexist, racist
teachers and by Evil Genius, who commanded them all. In
spite of its black and white analysis of American public
education, the play avoided an unrealistic happy ending.
Although the students organized and fought for change,
Evil Genius was only subdued, not eliminated.(41)

The Welfare Wizard of Ours grew into a short play
from an improvised skit prompted by legislative proposals
regarding welfare spending. Based directly on the Wizard
of Oz, the play examined the problems of the welfare
system, promoted socialism as the answer, and ended with
the newly united characters singing, "We're off to seize
the power/ the power that's rightfully ours." The play
shows the A & T's continual move away from specifically
feminist issues to social issues. However, it does focus on
a female protagonist and explores such issues as day care,
welfare mothers and the denigration of work done in the
home.(42)

Ally, Ally, All Come Free is another brief play which
was paired in performance with the company's version of
Brecht's The Exception and the Rule in 1973. Reviewer
Ann Payson says: "Ally, Ally, All Come Free is an improvisational statement about work in the home.... This
rather unsubstantial work makes some interesting comments
about life on the treadmill, but could use more bite."(43)

The musical satire Battered Homes and Gardens was
produced in 1974, and concerns a Minneapolis family
"trying to save their home from being demolished for an
urban renewal project."(44) Like The Welfare Wizard of
Ours, it grew from a skit, has a female protagonist and
devotes considerable attention to women's issues. According to Jan Mandell, "We dealt with female oppression but
also with class oppression. To us those issues were very
interrelated."(45)

Clown Wanted, produced in 1975, tackled unemployment with a mixture of song, dance, mime and acrobatics
via a plot about an unemployed woman who finds a job as a
clown. "Inflation causes her dismissal by an evil clown
boss,"(46) and she makes the rounds of employment and
unemployment offices. Eventually she returns to the clown
shop, organizes the other clowns and ousts the boss.(47)
Occasionally the protagonist was played by a black male
instead of a woman, changing the political focus from
sexism to racism.(48) The entertaining form and soft
political line were chosen to appeal to a broad segment of
the community (49), and the show was performed at hospitals, schools, cafes, parks, union picnics, churches and
unemployment offices.(50)

The overt, polemical content of the A & T's drama--
much of which came from the lives of the writer-performers
who were directly affected by urban renewal, welfare
problems, unemployment and sexism (51)--is a result of
the members' commitment to dealing with political issues
involving their community, their desire to expose and
eradicate human oppression, and their decision to perform

for less sophisticated audiences. Meri Golden says that
"the audience was always the key for us. We recognized
who our audience was and what they thought."(52)   Golden
also wrote, "The search for new forms, although important,
seemed less important to us than the search for new audiences which we felt required using popular forms infused
with new content."(53)

This eclectic style of musical comedy, use of Brechtian
devices, satire and episodic plots, was suited to the company's concerns and influenced by its portability, which
had put some theatrical forms out of reach. Lack of funds
and the desire to be accessible contributed to its technical
modesty. Its style and form were also influenced by the
fact that some shows were designed for rallies and outdoor
gatherings, which necessitated brevity.

From a feminist point of view it appears that the A &
T's drama moved from portraying specific women's issues,
as in Pig in a Blanket, to issues of a humanist or socialist
nature, as in Battered Homes and Gardens. As Jan Mandell pointed out, however, the plays, with the exception of
some performances of Clown Wanted, always revealed the
woman's point of view through the protagonists who were
always female.   "Urban renewal and welfare are feminist
issues."(54)

Audiences apparently agreed with Mandell's statement
because about 70 percent of each audience was feminist.
Audience feedback, so important to the group, was obtained through post-performance discussion which identified
the audience for the performers and provided criticism of
its work. Meri Golden says that the usual A & T audience
was predominantly white, middle or working class, aged 20
to 40 years and not made up of theatregoers. An equal
balance of women and men was usual, although a performance for a specific event could influence that ratio. The
A & T estimates it performed for 5000 people a year with
an average audience of a hundred. Seen in a wide variety
of places by Minneapolis residents, the company conducted
numerous tours throughout the midwest.(55)

Audiences everywhere were receptive to the A & T
and reviews were favorable. Reviews, however, were
rarely forthcoming from the major newspaper critics, possibly because of the large number of fringe theatres in
Minneapolis.   However, media attention is not always
proportional to artistic excellence; many theatres consistently reviewed consistently receive negative reviews.
(Small theatres, especially political and ethnic ones, generally begin to receive more media attention as they gain
establishment approval and/or achieve financial solvency.)
The A & T's principal media coverage came from alter-

native, political and women's publications, although it was
sporadically reviewed by the larger Minneapolis newspapers
and members of the collective appeared on several television talk shows.

The media which did cover A & T performances frequently commented on the performers' tremendous energy
and acting expertise, but noted needs for tightening up
scene shifts and for providing characters with more depth.
Some reviews expressed surprise that the politics in A & T
productions did not inhibit the art. A Dayton, Ohio,
review of Battered Homes and Gardens says, "Does it work
as theatre? Yes, to a remarkable degree.... On the
whole it moves in a zany, adroit manner and rarely becomes drably polemical."(56) Another review says:

> Just as powerful as the message in this production
> are the means used to convey it. The People Are
> a River is a well-executed combination of dialogue,
> music, dance, and visual effects to make the show
> fast-moving, funny and interesting.(57)

The A & T, admittedly less artistically successful
than it desired to be, was in the process of improving
performance skills when the troupe disbanded in 1976. Its
level of competence is related to the group's admission of
unskilled performers, lack of money for training, insis-
tence on the collective process and emphasis on political
content. The company, however, believed its political
messages could best be manifested in art, and it is reasonable to assume that if it had survived, its artistic level
would have continued to rise.

Politically the A & T was very successful if such
success can be measured by audience response. Its methods of working with political organizations and its high
accessibility put it in a position to have immediate social
impact. It is impossibe to determine if the A & T's work
directly influenced socially critical legislation, but some of
the success in defeating proposals that offended individual
members must be attributed to their activity as a company.
Their welfare plays may well have helped defeat Minnesota
Congressional Bill HR 1, "which would force welfare
mothers to work at 2/3 the minimum wage."(58) One
article on the company says, "They helped prevent a sta-
dium from gobbling a neighborhood; fought encroachment
by a shopping mart; helped marshal opinion against a
flossy apartment complex that is choking an inner-city
neighborhood."(59)

The A & T's success may be seen through its wide
influence on other political theatres, including the Lavender Cellar Theatre, the Circle of the Witch, the Wisconsin's People's Theatre, the Bertolt Brecht Theatre and the

Bread and Roses Theatre, for which it either served as a
model or helped organize.(60)

However, the A & T had a number of problems common to most small, political groups that work under frus-
trating conditions with little remuneration.   Attendant to
the financial difficulties was the lack of time to rehearse
and perform.   Since members had to work at other jobs to
support themselves, simply making a rehearsal schedule
which would include everyone was difficult.   In order for
the company to tour, members had to leave their jobs and
were unable to return to them after the tour.(61)

Another problem for the theatre was its attempt to
attract audiences of people who usually do not attend
theatre and who did not already agree with its message.
Playing in parks or neighborhood halls, often for free, did
not completely solve the problem.   In planning for this
ideal audience the group faced the dilemma of how politically subtle or obvious its drama should be.   This concern
was at the heart of the break-up of the company.

The break-up of the A & T was facilitated by a
political split in the group fostered by an outside organization called the Cooperative Organization that gained
considerable influence in many Minneapolis leftist groups.
The Cooperative Organization and A & T members who
affiliated with it demanded specific political content in
group plays and denigrated "theatre art" and the group's
collective process.(62)   This constituency, insisting on the
adoption of its methods and ideology, prompted an irrecon-
cilable split within the theatre company.   The A & T
disbanded at the time when it was creating a new play and
had just received a substantial grant.   Half of the company, incorporating new members, completed the A & T's
scheduled bookings under the name People's Holiday Theatre.   After six months this group dispersed.(63)   The
Cooperative Organization disappeared soon after, leaving
some former A & T members thinking that their theatre
had been sabotaged by a group designed to erode leftist
organizations.(64)

That the Cooperative Organization was able to under-
mine the A & T's activities indicates that the theatre did
not at the time hold a sufficiently unified political position.
Jan Mandell comments:

> We were fighting over different political points.
> This kind of thing seems to be a pattern in leftist
> groups in periods of low-key activism as the
> 1970's were compared to the 1960's.   Groups start
> blaming each other for the apparent failure and
> fall apart.(65)

Their arguments, instead of being productive as before,

were destructive. Becoming personal attacks, they created
enough bad feelings that members were unable to reconcile
themselves.

A review of the five years of Alive and Trucking
history reveals both a political and artistic evolution. The
company continued to perform agitprop pieces and guerrilla
theatre throughout its existence because it was adept at
creating these portable shows which provided alternate and
complementary forms of expression. By constantly seeking
new audiences who did not already agree with its political
position, the A & T assumed a revolutionary function.

As they endured, their theatrical expertise improved
and their drama moved from simple presentations of socioeconomic problems to more sophisticated, multi-layered
renderings which gave the audiences an experience capable
of inspiring social change.

Politically, the group gradually moved from a specifically feminist orientation to a socialist-feminist one, beginning in 1972, with the decision to include both men's
and women's history in The People Are a River. Over this
decision two women left the group feeling that its feminist
orientation was being undermined; the play-in-progress
when the break-up occurred was about the economy and
for the first time had a male lead.(66) Former A & T
members were uncertain about the reasons for their political change, but it is reasonable to suggest that the
company wished to include a broader spectrum of political
issues in performance. Some all-women companies, including Circle of the Witch and At the Foot of the Mountain, suggest that mixed theatre groups have a propensity
toward this response because the male members eventually
want to explore experiences and issues that are not specifically female or feminist. The artistic and political evolution of the A & T can best be seen by comparing its
first group-created, full-length play, Pig in a Blanket,
with one of its final works, Battered Homes and Gardens.

The introduction to Pig in a Blanket says that the
collectively written, produced and directed play came from
the authors' own experiences and is aimed at people much
like themselves--young, white, middle class and college
educated. It adds, however, that they do not think these
are the only people Pig in a Blanket speaks to, and that
the script "does not give an adequate idea of the play
since so much depends on the actors' movements and
characterizations" (p.7).(67) While script inadequacies are
present in any drama, the caution is necessary here because of the play's many dance and mime scenes, its
partially improvised scenes and its scenes which require
audience participation.

Pig in a Blanket, subtitled "A tender, poignant drama about young love," is arranged in two acts with eight scenes in the first and ten in the second. The play begins with the cast of eight miming the building of a sculpture which represents their play. Adding and subtracting from the imaginary art object amidst squabbles over design, they eventually reach an artistic consensus. Again reflecting their collective work process, they brainstorm for a title and decide on Pig in a Blanket. The dialogue and mime were different at each performance, but the title was always the same.

Scene Two, following the blackout which separates all scenes, presents three subsequent vignettes of working women--a janitor, a stewardess and a secretary--in their oppressive work environments. The scene comically and satirically examines job sex-role stereotyping and ends with a surrealistic finale in which a wedding parody is danced in a Hollywood 1950's style by the women and their bosses.

Scene Three is a dance-mime to the song "I Am Woman, You Are Man" about male-female relationships and stereotyped masculinity and femininity. Three couples dance and mime the song's lyrics emphasizing sex-role traits, but after each of three sounds of a gong, completely alter their style indicating changes in the relationships.

In order to expose human couplings, groupings and power plays, actors in Scene Four assume the identities of apes in a colony and mime all the usual social patterns, culminating in a fight among three male apes over a female. With the prize awarded to the winner, the apes slowly transform into Barbie and Ken dolls.

> The impression of the transition is that the apes are forced somehow to stand erect. They struggle against it ... [and] the last part of the body to transform is the face which becomes that of a doll--forced smile, glazed eyes. Their voices and movements are mechanical [pp. 19-20].

Three couples of Barbie and Ken converse in non sequiturs, one couple at a time repeating the same lines.

Barbie: I have a bikini.

Ken: We can ride in my Malibu.

Barbie: Do you want to go steady?

Ken: It's got 423 cubic inches, overhead cam.

Barbie: I can wear your ring.

Ken: Fuel injected ... [p. 20].

As the Barbies rattle on about feminine things and the Kens about masculine ones, they all gradually begin to behave like short-circuited robots jumbling and repeating lines and syllables. The chaos is ended by a blackout.

Scene Five suddenly sobers the performance with a stylized enactment of a gang rape of one actress. The male-female segregated audience was usually quite moved, and at some performances the rape was halted by audience women.(68)

"Rape" is followed by "The Bedroom" in which a post-coitus conversation expresses typical male-female guilt transference--she fakes orgasms; he ignores her at parties; she will not talk to him; he cannot talk to her.

Recitations of excerpts from Edgar Lee Masters' Spoon River Anthology form Scene Seven. Included are "Nellie Clark" and "Minerva Jones," who were sexually exploited and abused.

Act One ends with a pick-up of Scene Six in the bedroom, where the antagonized couple's disharmony is reflected in their inability to find one another in the room. Almost dreamlike they grope as if blind, call out for each other, becoming more and more panicked, as the song "Two Different Worlds" fades and the lights go out.

Act Two starts with a mime of two women who are kept apart by invisible barriers and finally find themselves trapped together in an imaginary box from which they are unable to escape.

Thematically similar to Scene One, scenes two through eight show the effects of socialization and restrictive roles. In Scene Two the company dances to Greek music in various groupings but are interrupted three times by a loudspeaker which defines a correct love relationship. Groups are eliminated one by one until only a female-male couple remain dancing. They too are divided by the last announcement which includes matrimony as a requirement for union.

Scene Three is a dance-mime of the birth and growth of a man. His joy for life, however, is interrupted by offstage derisive laughter which continues until he, failing to escape it, crouches paralyzed.

In the next scene an actor is continually subjected to substitutions--briefcase for purse, Marlboros for Virginia Slims, Playboy for poetry--and finally is given a white expressionless mask like that of everyone else.

Scene Five is a slide show picturing examples of the male macho image accompanied by a lecture on the disease "AMS"--American Male Sexuality. The point is that this behavior is learned and difficult to fight.

This image is again repudiated in the next scene,
which presents a narration of the Superman myth interspersed with dialogue and mime. Superman, the paradigm
of American male machismo, and his admirers, the Ken
dolls from Act One, Scene Four, end the scene in a spasm
of male power exhibitionism.

Women as victims of their socialization is the subject
of Scene Seven as a group of school girls malign each
other over John, the boy who claims to favor each.
Reality shifts to dreamlike introspection as the girls individually examine their hatred and finally join together
saying, "Who cares about John anyway?" (p. 40).

"Carnival," Scene Eight, groups several characters
from former scenes in a sideshow with Superman as the
barker who describes the special perversitites of each. As
Superman goes on to describe more creatures inside the
tent, those outside slowly join forces and seize him. In a
wash of red light the villain is twirled over their heads as
if on a runaway merry-go-round while the calliope music
swells.

With the villain at least momentarily subdued, Scene
Ten slows the pace with a simple poem by Ho Chi Minh
which speaks of rebirth after struggle and is read in
darkness.

To end the play the company used either of two
scenes, both requiring audience particiapation. Ending
one repeats Scene Two of Act Two except that this time no
voice stops the dancing, and the audience is invited to
join. In ending two the cast sits in the dark as the
spiritual, "Great Day," is played by one instrument.
Gradually more instruments and then voices come in as the
lights come up. Those in the audience, who have the
song lyrics in the programs, are invited to join the celebratory singing. After the company wrote the second
ending, a selection was made on the basis of knowledge
about each audience. The A & T, however, was never
completely satisfied with either ending. "No one ending
worked consistently. At times the dancing seemed to
inhibit the audience..." (p. 47). Both endings led directly
into a discussion of the play and performance.

Audience participation, always unpredictable, was
included by the A & T in an attempt to remove barriers
between audiences and actors and involve the community it
hoped to serve. However, as Richard Schechner, whose
Performance Group extensively uses audience involvement,
has pointed out, audience participation is often awkward
because the audience is not a community and in two hours
cannot be made into one.(69) Giving power to an audience
can come through altering subsequent performances based

on audience feedback; however, patrons can only see their influence if they return to a later performance. The A & T had greater success with audience participation when performing for groups, especially neighborhood organizations, which had common interests such as urban renewal problems.

During the year that Pig in a Blanket was performed, audiences were overwhelmingly enthusiastic about it. Women audience members were especially pleased to see issues relevant to them presented on the stage in an essentially woman-defined drama, but men were also positive in their comments during post-performance discussions. The play is anti-male only if one considers the current sexist status quo to be desirable. Scenes that attack the male image also point out why men adopt this role and how it ultimately restricts men, and these scenes oppose others (Three and Four in Act II) which show the male as victim. While the A & T may have intended to shock people into thinking in new ways, it was not intent on alienating its audience. The theme of unity suggests that the goals of feminism, if realized, will benefit both men and women.

Men and women were not, however, permitted to view Pig in a Blanket together. Audiences were either all female or if mixed, seated apart. The Alive and Trucking company, as well as many other feminist theatre groups, were aware of how different responses from women were when men were not in the audience. "Certain material played in a mixed context comes off one way. But in the context of only women, it comes off in a much deeper, more penetrating way."(70)

Since the A & T was a mixed theatre and Pig in a Blanket dealt with male and female issues of sexual politics, the company tried to get some of their audiences to respond without the inhibition of the presence of the opposite sex. Jan Mandell says that the technique was "pretty radical for 1972, but few people objected to the split."(71) Thus the audience participation in the final scene became a true dynamic of the production.

The sexual politics of Pig in a Blanket, while overt, never descend to screaming indictments. The liberal use of mime in the drama prevents heavy-handed didacticism because the concise art of mime itself proffers subtlety. The oppression which women face--job discrimination, sex-role stereotyping, rape, the beauty standard and abortion laws--are treated in a balance of comedy and seriousness to articulate the play's major themes of the often negative results of culturalization, codified behavior patterns based on sex and the inability of people to unite to fight their oppressors.

The non-linear form is unified by theme, scene repe-
titions and the reappearance of characters from previous
scenes.   The eclectic style, employing parody, transformation, dance, music, mime, realism, narrative, media presentation, fantasy, dream and poetry, is structurally divided by blackouts which effectively punctuate the vignettes
and work almost cinematographically to shift and stop the
stage action.

The show is greatly enhanced by technical assistance
of light and sound, but requires a minimal set.   Hand
props are used, but mood and environment are created by
the actors costumed in basic leotards and tights outfits to
which are added appropriate accessories.

The brief scenes allow little characterization, and
mime and dance expertise is as important as acting skill.
It appears that much of the play's vibrancy is related to
the actor-writers' personal involvement with their content.
Jan Mandell says, "The play grew from our own experiences, was about things · we understood, and had a truly
alive, believable quality."(72)

After Pig in a Blanket the A & T did not produce
another feminist play but rather created social dramas with
feminist   elements.   Battered Homes and Gardens,   the
company's last full-length play, was considered by some
members to be its best production because it successfully
combined pure entertainment with social messages and
because the company could see the direct results of its
efforts in the form of action taken by communities to halt
urban renewal.(73)

Battered Homes and Gardens was the A & T's first
original play with consistent plot and characters.   A
musical-comedy   satire,   it   selectively   includes   dance,
Brechtian devices, rhyming stichomythia, juggling, a slide
show and audience sing-alongs, to show in an entertaining
way the "impersonality of urban renewal and the way
clearing and rebuilding schemes cause trouble for the
people they displace."(74)

After a rousing song-and-dance number set at a
Minneapolis city planner's convention, which explains and
exposes the point of view of profit-hungry planners, the
action shifts to the Holmes' home in South Minneapolis.
Following the exposition in which one learns that Doris
(Mom), an oppressed housewife, and Jackie, her oppressed
teenage daughter, are ruled by Dad, who is pretty much a
product of male chauvinist culture, the news of the im-
pending urban renewal project, Looming Environmental Site
or LES, is disclosed.   Before the threatened residents
have time to react, the action switches to the LES backers,
Max A. Million and Phoebe Rhinequist, who detail their

plan's workings.   Conveniently Sally, Max A. Million's secretary, is Doris' married daughter, and Sally's unemployed husband Tom, is going to be hired as an LES planner.

While Phoebe is not essential to the story, she is nevertheless interesting because while she verbally identifies herself with the women's movement, in actuality she is mostly concerned with making it in the male business world.   Meri Golden says that some people criticized the image of Phoebe, but that "we felt we had to deal with a certain bourgeois, false image of feminism and disclaim it."(75)   In spite of the criticism, the character of Phoebe was not altered.

Back at the Holmes', Dad has been to a neighborhood meeting but feels powerless to stop the demolition of his house.   A neighbor, George, reinforces the hopelessness, but the girls, Jackie and her friend Beth, convince Mom that they have to organize and fight city hall.   As the trio solicits signatures on a petition, they encounter a range of responses from neighbors who are apathetic, feel resistance is useless, and consider petitions akin to communism, to those who are willing to sign.   They do finally get enough names, and in the process Mom has changed from a self-deprecating housewife to a militant organizer.

The plot builds through more scenes relating the complexity of the conflicts and climaxes at a public hearing. Max A. Million's sales pitch for LES culminates in a slide show presenting his vision of the city.   Tom, however, has been won over by his wife Sally and her family and has switched the slides.   As Max, with his back to the screen, narrates his dream, the photos reveal destroyed neighborhoods, bulldozed homes and towers of glass, steel and cement.   Max A. Million says:

> This exciting dynamic process will soon bring convenience to your doorstep.   (Slide of a house's doorstep being torn away.)
> Our city is on the move!   (Slide of a house being moved.)(76)

The Holmes' neighborhood is saved through their efforts, but in the A & T's desire to be realistic, the ending is not all happy.   LES is now being proposed for an adjacent area where George lives.

Reviews of Battered Homes and Gardens consistently praised the production, noting especially the many clever songs, most of which were original.   Still others parodied well-known tunes.   As in most musicals the characters lacked depth, but except for the villains, they were not one-dimensional stereotypes.

>The show probably represents too unsympathet-
>ically the motives of developers and planners
>whom it tends to parody. But it well humanizes
>the reactions to renewal suggestions of many
>people both in favor and oppposed.(77)

Reviewer Peter Altman also felt the play dwelt too much on
"peripheral issues such as women's rights, parent-child
relationships and Wounded Knee."(78) Jan Mandell points
out that the oppressions of Mom, the main character,
Jackie, Beth and the other women were very interwoven
with the urban renewal crisis.(79) The reviewer thought
these things got in the way.

The play was written for the practical purpose of
helping to inform and agitate people threatened by Minneapolis' many urban renewal projects and as such provides
an effective illustration of the "process by which a power
grab that menaces a neighborhood can be defeated."(80)
Jan Mandell comments:

>One important thing in Battered Homes and Gar-
>dens is showing how a character changes, what
>makes a person move from an attitude of hope-
>lessness or cynicism to one of wanting to act. We
>hoped that when people left the theatre they
>thought about that and the possibility of their
>lives' being changed. A big part of coming to
>the A & T, as characterized by the song "You're
>Not Alone," was to find out that the feelings you
>have are shared by others.(81)

Battered Homes and Gardens was played in many
Minneapolis neighborhoods and is full of local color and
lines that can be changed to suit a specific locale. When
the show was toured in the Midwest it was canceled in
Dayton, Ohio, because the Dayton Art Institute, where it
was to be performed, reneged on lending its facilities.

>The Dayton Art Institute had agreed to lend its
>auditorium for a Friday performance and had even
>put out a glowing press release about the Alive
>and Trucking troupe. But after a University of
>Dayton performance earlier in the week, the mu-
>seum suddenly remembered that its charter pro-
>hibits "political groups."
>Some parties to the squabble are saying the
>museum's memory was jogged by city hall.
>Gail Levin, city commissioner, admits she saw
>the theatre company's flyer, noted that some
>comments were decidedly anti-Dayton, and felt
>they should be called to the attention of museum
>personnel. But she claims that "no strong-arm

pressure was applied in order to have the performance canceled."(82)
The show went on at the Dayton First Unitarian Church
and amidst all the controversy, played to packed houses.
    The juxtaposition of Pig in a Blanket and Battered
Homes and Gardens reveals the group's propensity for
popular forms which it felt were best suited to its audiences. Jan Mandell explains, "it's not that we thought
people were stupid, but abstract forms require a certain
degree of theatre exposure or education which working
class people in America usually do not have."(83) It also
seems significant that if a theatre wants its audience to
act, it should not make them work to perceive the message.
    Battered Homes and Gardens, although incorporating
a variety of circus skills, represents a change in group
playwriting technique. Previous group collaborations had
taken the revue or skit form, and certainly the ideas in
Battered Homes and Gardens could have been similarly
molded. The drama can be viewed as a progression in
playwriting skill for the collective because it was able to
coordinate its talents to create defined characters in a
linear plot, a more difficult task than writing an episodic
plot or series of vignettes. Evidence suggests that the
theatre was learning more about playwriting and about how
to coordinate the writing skills of the group. Equally
important is the fact that the A & T had developed a style
of musical comedy which included its members' special talents such as mime, dance, juggling and acrobatics and was
able to deliver a message in an entertaining form that
audiences liked.
    Pig in a Blanket, specifically feminist, deals with the
theoretical and all-encompassing problem of sexism. Battered Homes and Gardens, feminist only in the broadest
sense of the word, deals with the narrower problems of
urban renewal. In some performances it focused on specific Minneapolis projects. The first play is far less
portable than the second, and the audience for Battered
Homes and Gardens was much broader. Pig in a Blanket
is a more serious play than Battered Homes and Gardens
although both encourage unity as the means to achieve
common good. Probably the difference in the two plays,
and thus the character of the A & T, is most related to its
apparent political shift from feminism to socialism. Indeed,
persons familiar with the A & T's work only since 1973,
are surprised to learn that the group considered itself a
feminist theatre.
    In its five years of operation the A & T managed to
perform hundreds of times for thousands of persons, and

its style and collective structure served as a model for
many other political groups. With little financial or emotional support other than that from audiences, it ran on
energy and commitment, making a lot from very little.
Above all the company showed that socio-political theatre
could have impact and please an audience at the same time.

Chapter III

THE LAVENDER CELLAR THEATRE

The Lavender Celler Theatre, founded in Minneapolis in 1973, and currently inactive, was a lesbian-feminist theatre.

The rights and oppressions of lesbians are deep concerns of the women's movement because "lesbianism, like male homosexuality, is a category of behavior possible only in a sexist society characterized by rigid sex roles."(1) A lesbian-feminist theatre differs from a gay theatre, such as Minneapolis' Out and About Theatre, in that most gay theatres focus on male homosexuality while lesbian-feminist theatres focus on female homosexuality and have aligned themselves with the feminist movement.

The feminist movement attracted many lesbians. "Oppressed both for their sex and for their sexual preference, such women saw the need for organization and action."(2) At first both the movement and lesbians played down the lesbian issue, believing it would hurt the cause of women's liberation. However, with increasing gay consciousness in the late 1960's, lesbian women active in women's groups became less willing to remain hidden.

Under pressure, the women's movement did accept the lesbian's cause. The Fifth Annual Conference of the National Organization for Women in 1971, resolved the following:

> That NOW recognizes the double oppression of women who are lesbians. That a woman's right to her own person includes the right to define and express her own sexuality and to choose her own lifestyle. That NOW acknowledges the oppression of lesbians as a legitimate concern of feminism.(3)

This view was overwhelmingly supported again in November 1977 at the National Women's Conference in Houston, Texas.

While most feminists are not lesbians, any consideration of a lesbian-feminist group must recognize the interrelationship of the two elements. Lavender Cellar defined

43

itself as a lesbian-feminist theatre to emphasize the lesbian
aspect of feminist theatre.

The theatre was primarily the idea of Marie Kent,
who, inspired by the work of the Alive and Trucking
Theatre, organized a group of women at the Minneapolis
Lesbian Resource Center to form a permanent theatre
collective. The formation was motivated by a desire to
explore theatrically and validate the lesbian experience and
by the need for an artistic voice in the lesbian community.(4) Nythar Sheehy says, "The lesbian-feminist community was hungry for any kind of social activity and for
seeing their emotions and experiences presented on the
stage." The theatre functioned as a support group for its
members and its community. Besides its therapeutic function, Lavender Cellar created an environment for women to
come together and share theatre skills.

Lacking role models for a lesbian-feminist theatre and
fearing social rejection, the group floundered, unable to
stabilize its membership. The women considered joining
the Alive and Trucking Theatre but did not because that
group would have been unable to devote enough attention
to lesbian issues. Indeed, by 1973, Alive and Trucking
was moving away from even specifically feminist issues.(5)

In September 1973 the group again attempted to form
a theatre, but this time it proposed a less threatening
organization and a collective structure. The Lavender
Cellar was to be open to any lesbian-feminist who could
devote time and energy to one production. It aimed primarily to raise consciousnesses and develop talent through
ingroup performances for the Minneapolis lesbian
community.

Eventually a core group of eight women, few of whom
had experience in theatre, formed. Realizing its artistic
limitations and that developing theatrical skills is a long
process, the group realistically adjusted its artistic goals.
Marie Kent states, "Although we were aware of the need
for artistic development, we were more concerned about
presenting our experience for other gay women." Member
Karen Hanson [see note 4] adds:

> The lesbian community was very small and non-
> cohesive in 1973. Just that we existed was a
> major accomplishment. We had to develop our own
> confidence to perform this kind of theatre before
> we could take it to the general public to educate
> or raise their consciousnesses.

The Lavender Cellar rehearsed and mostly performed
at the Lesbian Resource Center, which acted as a support
group and financial backer. The center, however, neither
directed nor restricted the theatre's activites.

The members adopted a collective structure because the Lesbian Resource Center was successfully run this way, and because the theatre wished to overcome "establishment theatre's management politics, competitiveness and hierarchies." Besides collective responsibility for all work and decisions, the group employed the process to handle personal problems and air members' feelings. Marie Kent says, "As we went along we worked through problems and conflicts so that the production proceeded without tension, and we could free ourselves to get into the play."

Collective administration worked well for the group possibly because it was small; the members were accustomed to working with each other; their productions, mostly pastiches or revues, were well suited to group direction; and the group had not expanded to the point of needing elaborate booking procedures, record keeping, transportation, technical equipment and publicity. However, with the production of Cory, the group's most ambitious undertaking, members noted that the collective process often seemed to inhibit progress and was unproductively time consuming. The occasional failure of the process in any group seems related to the way each group recognizes and utilizes individual skills and talents and sets up means for solving problems.

Financially, the theatre operated by borrowing money for each production from the Lesbian Resource Center, which kept a special Lavender Cellar account, and repaying from proceeds after the show closed. Admission, $2 by donation, was the group's only source of income, but it met expenses. Members were not paid; any profits went into its account to be used for the next production or for equipment purchases. (The chief group investment was $200 for a lighting system.)

The company rehearsed on an average of twice weekly, intensifying to five times a week for the three-week period preceding an opening. Methods of working varied with each show.

Any member could submit a script for consideration or offer ideas for a collaborative creation. Scripts were unsuccessfully solicited from outside sources such as the Washington Area Feminist Theatre clearinghouse.

Following readings and informal auditions, shows were cast and staff assigned by collective approval. Play direction was also collaborative. "People explored parts as they interpreted them and the director was more of a coordinator. When a total interpretation was necessary, a discussion was held with the entire cast in an effort to pool ideas."(6) Rehearsals followed a somewhat traditional pattern, except for the collective decision making, and incorporated techniques of improvisation, physical and vocal exercise, emotional response and Gestalt therapy. Nythar Sheehy comments:

> We used emotional response and Gestalt exercises as a means of getting in touch with the feelings the characters were expressing which had also been our own feelings. Cory contained many experiences like frustration, anger and isolation that we all had had, and it got very heavy to deal with these and expose them on stage.

Clearly the process, inasmuch as it involved collectivity, skill sharing, therapy and risk taking, was as important to the Lavender Cellar as its final product. This process, begun with Prisons, was developed and refined through subsequent productions.

The first play, Prisons, a one-act by member Pat Suncircle, depicted the roles in which people are willingly and unwillingly cast and the consequences of defining one's role. Presented first at the Lesbian Resource Center in the spring of 1973, the portable production was kept in repertory and taken on tour to conferences and meetings.

In December 1973 the group performed an occasional piece, Scene at the Center, a musical parody reflecting interaction and activity at the Lesbian Resource Center. This piece, intentionally limited in its appeal, was only performed at the center.

In February 1974, the company performed, again at the Lesbian Resource Center, a modern dance revue, Isadora Is Arisen, coordinated by Nythar Sheehy. In May, it presented Women's Struggle Throughout History, a reader's theatre production based on the writings of such women as Sojourner Truth, Gertrude Stein and Susan B. Anthony. This show, revealing the group's concern for strong role models and for recapturing women's lost history, parallels similar efforts of other feminist theatres, including the Co-Respondents' Give 'Em an Inch, the Alive and Trucking's The People Are a River and Circle of the Witch's Time Is Passing.

In the fall of 1974, the group put together a musical revue of eight short acts titled Cabaret '74. Like Scene at the Center, it was a celebration of the lesbian experience, designed to entertain and provide a social basis of unity for the lesbian community.

As the group continued each production became more ambitious, possibly because members became more skilled and collectively efficient. Its final piece before becoming inactive, Cory, an in-progress work written by Pat Suncircle and presented in May 1975, was about a 16-year-old girl's struggle with family, friends, society and self in dealing with her lesbianism.

The cast of ten principals includes Cory Jergens, the teenage heroine; Captain Jergens, Cory's father, who cares for his daugher but cannot accept her lesbianism; Melinda Jergens, Cory's mother, who does not understand her daughter's withdrawn behavior and tries to foist an accepted role of sweet sixteen on her; Lt. Commander Denise McCleod, who works for Cory's father, is a friend to the girl and is herself secretly gay; Susan, who is a professed lesbian whose background in many ways parallels Cory's; and Mary Jane and Douglas, who are Cory's high school classmates.(7)

The two-act drama begins with Cory and Denise riding in a car chatting. By the eighteenth line it is clear that Cory is a lesbian and that her friend Denise has some special understanding of Cory's situation. Cory expresses her desire to publicly reveal her identity, but Denise reminds her of society's penalties.

Scene two begins as Cory leaves the car and joins her school classmates, Mary Jane and Doug, the latter of whom is attracted to and rejected by Cory. As the trio heads home their conversation revolves around school activities, centering on a psychology term paper on homosexuality which Cory plans to write. The scene reveals middle-class heterosexual teenager's ideas, fantasies and ignorance of homosexuality. Doug brags (p.6) that he and "some buddies busted up a gay bar"(8) and Mary Jane warns Cory to stay away from such bars in her research work because, "you'd get raped--by women!"(p. 6)

Scene Three switches the action to Denise's office on the military base where Mrs. Jergens is showing Denise the clothes she has purchased for Cory's upcoming birthday party. The mother has not a clue to her daughter's strange behavior and attributes it to Cory's thinking they have all forgotten her birthday. Captain Jergens enters and discloses the problems he is having with the admiral. The captain throughout is portrayed as a well-meaning sort who is completely absorbed in the pressures of Navy business. Cory enters, others leave, and we again see Cory alone with Denise, who advises Cory to tell her parents about her lesbianism. Cory responds, "They'd put me away" (p. 10), which is in fact their response. The two exit, and their conversation is heard as if by eavesdropping against a background of Susan drudgingly going about her cleaning work in the office. Cory confesses to Denise that she is in love with her, and Denise kindly explains that she is not ready for such a relationship.

In Scene Five the surprise birthday party preparations are in progress. Eventually Cory arrives via a carload of drunken sailors, herself drunk, and collapses.

The party breaks up, and the scene fades into a mime of
Cory expressing her entrapment and rage on one half of
the stage while on the other, Susan pulls out the candles
on the cake one by one and tosses them into the trash.

Scene Six, titled Aftermath, is simultaneous in chron-
ology with the end of Scene Five and concerns Captain
Jergens explaining Cory's "sickness" to Doug. It seems
the school psychologist has betrayed Cory's confidence and
told her father that she is mentally ill--a lesbian. Doug
blames Denise's influence and recommends she be transferred. Captain Jergens' solution, however, involves
Doug. The Captain says:

> You know don't you that someday Cory is going
> to have a good husband and a home and children.
> Either that or a good job and boyfriends. She's
> going to love them very much and be happy as a
> complete woman.... Well, I just wish that right
> now she could know what it's going to be like.
> She should start to realize now about the man-
> woman relationship. Most girls already know at
> her age, and she would too, but the sickness....
> Well, I need your help.
> I'm not trying to set up anything, any perma-
> nent arrangement or anything, but I want you to
> help her. You see she trusts you, and you
> could--be alone with her for a time [p. 16].

Doug grudgingly agrees to the plan after the captain
promises to assist Doug in getting into Annapolis.

Act Two, Scene One, juxtaposes Cory and Susan with
a group of average teenagers in a teen hangout. This
encounter, like other brief previous ones, prepares for the
play's ending and develops the character of Susan.

Doug's attempt to seduce Cory in an apartment borrowed by the captain for this purpose follows. The seduction fails and ends in a physical fight culminating in the
arrival of Cory's father. Cory flees.

Cory returns to Denise after an indefinite absence,
recounts her adventures while away and again seeks
Denise's affection which she again refuses. Denise leaves
the office, and Susan appears offering Cory refuge from
her family who is searching for her. Susan reveals her
own past and how her parents found it more acceptable
that she was an unwed, pregnant 16-year-old than a
lesbian.

The play ends with Cory at Susan's apartment vowing
to confront her parents the next day. She explains her
feelings for Denise to Susan which involve "much more
than sex" (p. 27) and the lights dim on Susan's embracing
Cory.

While the play focuses on the character of Cory and her fear and frustration, it also deals with related aspects of the same problem through Denise, who has not come to terms with her homosexuality, and Susan, who has. Society's rejection and misunderstanding of lesbianism is shown through the students who giggle about it, the school psychologist who regards it as mental illness, the mother who cannot even discuss it and the father who believes that sexual intercourse with a male will cure it. Sex-role sterotyping is presented through Cory's parents who attempt to make a young lady of her and through Susan's parents who found motherhood under any circumstances preferable to lesbianism.

Cory does progress through the play to become a stronger person ready to own her new identity in spite of the difficulty she must face. It is unclear what Denise will do. The open ending was deliberately chosen by the playwright in order to stimulate discussion afterward. Her introduction to the play says that "it is an educational play open to interpretation and when produced should be accompanied by open discussion after each performance." Suncircle's play is partially autobiographical and partially "from the experiences of several young gay women whom I have talked to" (Introduction).

While the play is realistic and its narrative chronological, the action shifts rapidly from one place to another, and the length of time lapses is often unclear. This time-place jumping indicates the writer's desire for transformational techniques which allow smooth progression without naturalistic preparation. The 11 scenes move rapidly in a rising and falling fashion; there is no one climax which would be expected in a play about a girl who is deciding how to reveal that she is lesbian. Rather the play builds, first, to Cory's confession of love for Denise, second, to the birthday party episode, third, to the near rape in the apartment and, last, to the main character's almost accidental discovery of Susan, a woman who will understand and comfort her. The anticipated child-parent confrontation scene never takes place. The tension is maintained by preparing each action carefully with the preceding one.

Suncircle's diction and dialogue well capture the language rythms of her characters and avoid popular phrases and epithets which ultimately date a play.

The two-act play, which runs about an hour and a half, is too brief to fully develop its multitude of characters, and thus many in Cory are stereotypes. However, Suncircle avoided making her characters caricatures. For example, the father is not portrayed as an evil man, but as a product of his culture, who has typical responses to his child's being a homosexual. Inasmuch as he cares for his daughter there is the possibility that he will come to understand her.

The drama, however, fails to explain some things. How Cory knows that Denise is gay, when Denise herself can hardly admit it, is unclear and a weakness of the plot because the relationship of these two women dominates the dramatic action. Why the father suddenly appears at the apartment during the seduction scene is confusing. Did he have second thoughts about his plan, or is his arrival merely a device to allow Cory to see his participation in the contrivance? The first scene of Act Two in the teen-age hangout seems unnecessary because it imparts no new information or insight. It appears to be a device to permit Cory and Susan an additional encounter and to get the play started again after the intermission. Cory's returning to Denise's office after running away seems contrived since the script states that the naval base has been mobilized to aid in the search for her.

Whatever its dramatic weaknesses, Cory is a sensitve play which deals with issues rarely presented in the the-atre. While political, it is only mildly didactic and illus-trates the problems lesbian women face. Coupled with discussion afterwards, Cory provides a much-needed outlet and experience for lesbian women. Indeed, such perfor-mances foster communal identity and better fulfill the unique functions of live theatre than do most professional productions.

Technically the play indicates a need for area lighting and minimal, suggestive sets as its locations rapidly change from automobile to sidewalk to office to home to drugstore and to apartment. This design was in fact employed in the Lavender Cellar's production.

The roles of the men in this production were played by women wearing men's costumes; it is impossible to judge if this worked without seeing it. Although no one in the audience objected to it, it seems very clear to me that allowing men to play all the men's roles would render the play a more accurate and realistic presentation. Nowhere does Suncircle indicate that it was her intention to have the male roles played by women. However, the all-woman company wished to perform the play and was unwilling to include men in the cast.

The drama, which was well received by the predom-inantly gay audience, fulfills the Lavender Cellar's objec-tive of presenting the lesbian experience. However, the efficacy of the production depends on the spectator's empathy for or identification with lesbianism.

Discussions following performances, the only criticism the group received since it was not reviewed by the media, examined the plays and facilitated analysis of lesbian issues and gay rights. Nythar Sheehy says that the main criticism of the theatre's work concerned the audience's desire for more depth, more radical political content and longer pieces.

Since the group only performed its gay material for gays or gay sympathizers, it received no criticism from neutral or anti-gay people. Its play, Prisons, about sex-role stereotyping, was the only play performed for a predominantly heterosexual audience.

Performance runs at the Lesbian Resource Center and tours exposed about 2000 people to the six presentations of the Lavender Cellar in its two-year existence.(9) Performances can be classified neither as revolutionary nor agitprop since they were neither attempting to change public attitudes nor merely to present overt propagandistic skits. The company's form and content sought to entertain and portray lesbianism for lesbians. The choice of an in-group audience was actually more of a response to the realities of social pressure than to the sort of political position adopted for example by some black theatres that perform only for blacks. The group found performing only for the gay community rewarding and important work, but it sees the possibility, if it reorganizes, of expanding its efforts to include public performances.

Company members relate their current inactivity to a lack of time and money. Karen Hanson says, "Time and money are related because if you didn't have to hold a job outside the theatre, there would be time." In 1975, after working on Cory for five months, the group's energy waned, and the members decided to become inactive. Marie Kent says that, "The core group was exhausted, and new energy was not forthcoming."

With the exception of Pat Suncircle, the core group stayed in the Minneapolis area, entertaining hopes to reorganize. The members believe that now they would be able to perform more outside the Lesbian Resource Center and that since the lesbian community has grown considerably, they would have even more support and interest. Improving theatre skills and writing and/or performing better plays would be future aims. Marie Kent says:

> I think that if we were to start today there'd be more focus on the art of the theatre. Also now we wouldn't be so fragmented with our own consciousness raising. There is definitely a need for lesbian-feminist theatre in Minneapolis.

It appears that the main success of the Lavender
Cellar Theatre came from giving emotional and intellectual
support to those who already agreed with its position.
Michael Kirby comments on the value of such theatre:

> Just as a marching band helps to stir the soldier's
> patriotism, courage, and spirit, political theatre
> can be the rallying point for the believers in a
> particular cause. It can give them the feeling
> that they are not alone in their beliefs, that
> others are actively involved and pursuing the
> same goals. Thus, it can be an important force
> in political change.(10)

Chapter IV

CIRCLE OF THE WITCH

Circle of the Witch, a "Collective Feminist Theatre," was founded by four women in Minneapolis in the fall of 1973 to explore the relationship between theatre and feminism. After exchanging ideas and experiences through theatrical improvisations for two months, the women formed a theatre company and chose Circle of the Witch as its name. The word circle in the title refers to "a female symbol of roundness, eggs, ovaries, and a universal symbol of communication and cooperation";(1) witch refers to "our link with a matriarchal past, a time in which men and women shared equally in a cooperative society."(2) The group was generally influenced by the radical theatre movement and specifically by the Alive and Trucking Theatre which helped the group get started by attending early rehearsals and lending support. Two of the founders of Circle of the Witch had formerly worked with the A & T.(3)

The all-women theatre, whose membership averaged seven in number, was composed of white women in their twenties from middle- or working-class backgrounds. In contrast to both the A & T and the Lavender Cellar, a majority of the women had experience or training in theatre, although such experience was not a requirement for joining.(4) Women interested in joining the collective usually attended several workshops where mutual compatibility was tested. After such an initiation period, women wishing to join had to make a year's commitment to the theatre, although full and part-time affiliation was possible.(5) The company intensified its efforts to recruit women from minority backgrounds in order to present a fuller perspective of the woman's experience.(6)

Men were not invited to join Circle of the Witch because the group wished to focus on women's issues and experiences and discover the kind of art women might create away from male influence, which explains why the founders did not simply join the Alive and Trucking.

Power was also an issue in the decision. Micki Massimino, one of the founders, said that since women are
unaccustomed to exerting power and men are accustomed,
in mixed groups men usually end up running things.(7)
Members also noted from their experiences in other theatres not only that males tended to dominate, but that less
skill sharing occurred. Product rather than process
oriented, the men in such theatres reasoned that sharing
jobs, skills and responsibilities was inefficient and time
wasting.(8)

Joyce Indelicato said that if men were admitted to the
group, every aspect of the work would radically change
because the dynamics of mixed groups differ considerably
from all-female or all-male groups. "The personal aspects
of our theatre are very important, and I think we'd lose
that quality if men joined us."(9)

The decision to exclude men was paralleled by many
feminist theatres, including the Rhode Island Feminist
Theatre which changed from a mixed group to an all-female
group, at least in part for the reasons given by Massimino
and Indelicato.(10) Some groups wishing to perform plays
which require a male have compromised by including a male
performer for that production only as At the Foot of the
Mountain did in 1977 with The Moon Tree.(11)

The Circle of the Witch's philosophy of a feminist
theatre involved its ideas on art, politics and audience.

> By cooperating together in the development of
> artistic pieces, we hope to challenge those in-
> grained ideas which support today's society and
> to learn new ways of thinking and seeing the
> world around us. Our concern is to apply the-
> atre to the exploration of personal, artistic, and
> socio-economic matters.(12)

Circle of the Witch attempted to put personal themes and
activities within a larger political context.

> We say that all art is political meaning that all art
> makes a statement, whether in affirming the
> dominant society or in suggesting more humane
> ways to work and live. When we say that our art
> (which is our personal experience translated to a
> piece on stage) is political, we are saying that
> the personal is political. That is, our experiences
> have political and social value and meaning.(13)

Seeking working people, non-theatregoers and poorer
people for its audience, the theatre had to be highly
mobile. "Since most people in America don't go to the
theatre, it's part of our operational philosphy to go to our
audiences."(14)

In its 1974 brochure the collective listed its goals as:

> to create a supportive working environment; to
> clearly identify our enemies, e.g., sexism (not
> men), capitalism, imperialism; to give women back
> their herstory and a sense of pride in their past;
> to identify our struggles with those of other op-
> pressed people and to give us all a feeling of our
> true strength and mutual support; to give a
> positive alternative to everything negative we
> present; and to communicate these ideas through
> exciting theatre.

Circle of the Witch's philosphy and goals were imple-
mented by a collective group structure which is in itself a
reflection of group ideals. According to its 1975 brochure,

> Dissatisfaction with group dynamics in the past
> prompted us to choose a process we define as
> collective. We are leaderless, that is, we operate
> non-hierarchically, cooperating to combine the
> energies and skills of individuals who choose to
> work with us toward a common goal. Everyone
> has equal say in decision making in both business
> and artistic matters.

Collective responsibility extended to every aspect of
theatre work. The bulk of theatre business was handled
by a staff member who was paid $100 per month. This
business manager worked two days a week in the theatre
office. As an affiliate of the Southside Neighborhood Arts
Council, which assists small artistic groups, Circle of the
Witch rented office space for a minimal charge in the
Council's building.(15)

Adjunct business tasks of scrapbook keeping, filing,
van maintenance and publicity were done by individuals,
but these jobs also rotated. Even the position of director,
when such a position is designated, rotated among members
and was viewed as more of an artistic coordinator than
controller.

The collective budgeted its time among creating new
plays, revising and performing the current one, tending to
theatre business tasks and improving their collective process. To write a new play collectively, the troupe worked
for four to twelve months with a minimum of three meetings
per week in addition to a two-week intensive workshop.
While the new play was in progress and for some time after
its opening, the current play was performed an average of
once weekly.

Biweekly business meetings alternated with the basis-
of-unity meetings at which the group talked about personal,
collective, political and artistic goals and problems. These
sessions, designed to keep the group alert to its purpose,
permitted open discussion of almost anything and thus

served to preserve group harmony and to emphasize the importance of the collective's process.(6) Basis-of-unity meetings, although named otherwise, are held by all the Minneapolis feminist theatres for similar reasons. Such sessions have their roots in the consciousness-raising encounters of the women's movement and may be the most important factor in feminist theatre's success with collective operation.

The company kept records of most theatre activities in notebooks. Basis-of-unity meeting notes, general business meeting notes, new play notes and audience discussion notes allowed the group to know what it had done, from which it planned to proceed without repetition. Notes taken from audience-performer discussions frequently formed the basis for changing parts of plays.(17)

Circle of the Witch was incorporated as a non-profit organization with a yearly budget of about $10,000. Income came from ticket sales ($3 regular admission, $2 for students and $1 for senior citizens and unemployed); fees from hiring groups of $100 to $200 for the current production and $400 to $500 for the newest one; grants totaling $2,300 as of summer 1977; and various fund-raising projects. Besides production costs, the group paid for office rent, staff salaries, collective property maintenance and remuneration to actors who missed work in order to perform and who took classes for the purpose of teaching skills to the collective. While the group always met its expenses, it had hopes to pay its members more in the future by obtaining more grants.(18)

The collective worked wherever it could find free or low-cost rehearsal space, usually in a church or women's center. Its plays were all collectively created, although the members did say that they were open to doing a scripted work if they could find one that said what they want to say. Joyce Indelicato explained, "We work for hours deciding on every line in our own scripts, so it's hard to do somebody else's work without changing a lot in it."(19) Collective works inherently supplied suitable roles for each writer-performer, whereas outside scripts may not, or they may include male roles.

In addition to its plays, the group wrote and performed over a dozen occasional skits and guerrilla pieces on daycare, birth control, abortion, welfare, social work and the history of Mayday.(20)

To create a play, the group used a variety of theatre games, exercises and improvisation, but the process for each of the three plays varied.

Sexpot Follies, based on our lives and anger at our oppression, came out of a lot of personal discussion and improvisation. For Lady in the Corner we had moved beyond some of that anger and could focus on women--a mother and her two daughters--rather than our anger towards men. Time Is Passing was more intellectual as it involved extensive research on Minnesota women's history.(21)

A typical Circle of the Witch rehearsal-workshop involved, first, a gathering of the group in a circle to provide each member an opportunity to describe briefly her present state of mind. A deep relaxation exercise followed based on the yoga principle of stimulation through relaxation. A twenty-minute physical and vocal warmup preceded the operation of either working on the new play or revising the current one. In the former case several developmental exercises aimed at releasing the performer and ultimately increasing ensemble acting skill were done. Such exercises were developed by a group member who acted as facilitator for that exercise and combined experimental theatre techniques such as those used by Viola Spolin, Richard Schechner or the Open Theatre, with original activities created by the facilitator. Some workshop exercises were specifically designed to relate to the play's content, and the results of such work were often incorporated into the play.

In the company's Roots Game, for example, the group sat in a circle while one person at a time told a story about her cultural roots. As she talked, she beat out the story's rhythm on a drum. Others in the circle might become involved in the story through rhythmic sound and movement and ritualistically aid in its telling. Nancy Sugarman says that Roots was designed to help members learn more about each other's cultural past as well as develop ensemble interdependence. She adds that the exercises could become an abstract introduction of characters in a play.(22)

Joyce Indelicato said that many of the exercises directly copied from other theatres had different results when done by Circle of the Witch because its individual and group identity and political focus were different.(23) The group used improvisation techniques when a script was forming, but its use of exploratory or developmental exercises, although less directly translatable into a drama, may have had a deeper impact on its work and influence on its ensemble creating-performing abilities.

Perhaps the main difference between a collective and non-collective theatre is that the former emphasizes cooperation rather than competition. Practically, this attitude produces a secure environment where actors are free to

take risks and be vulnerable without fear. Pressure is
relieved and individuals can teach and learn knowing that
because there are no stars or leaders, their ideas will be
heard and tested. In competitive, hierarchical theatres
that are less democratic cooperation is rare, frequently to
the point that each person considers only herself or him-
self and rehearsals are merely a means to an end.

Circle of the Witch shows were performed in rented
spaces in Minneapolis such as the Firehouse Theatre or the
Walker Church and ran for about seven weekends. After
such a run, shows were available for hire throughout the
Midwest and were performed at universities, public schools,
women's conferences, union gatherings, community centers,
prisons, senior citizens' centers, food cooperatives and
parks.(24)

An understanding of Circle of the Witch's evolving
performance style and content can best be obtained by
examining its three plays, Sexpot Follies (1974), Lady in
the Corner (1975), and Time Is Passing (1976).

Sexpot Follies, structurally akin to the vaudeville
revue, opens with a song-and-dance curtain raiser. The
mistress of ceremonies, who keeps the vignettes moving,
introduces the cast who then sings a parody of "I'm a
Little Teapot," called "I'm a Little Sexpot." Verses of this
song are repeated throughout the play. The play is
composed of monologues and realistic and abstract scenes
of dialogue which focus on feminist issues of the beauty
standard, sex-role stereotyping, female manipulation,
mother-daughter relationships, exploitation of working
women and rape.

The rape scene begins as a sexual assault on the MC.
The masked, cloaked rapists move in, then freeze as rape
statistics are quoted over a loudspeaker. Each rapist then
removes a hood identifying an institution which "rapes"
women--government, mass media, education, the nuclear
family and institutionalized religion--and describes how it
operates. The forces undergo a transformation, and,
while removing masks, voice an alternative method of
fulfilling society's needs without exploiting women. The
Alternative Family says:

> We are the re-defined family. Our survival is no
> longer based on the exploitation of our members.
> We represent the freedom to choose your own
> living arrangements--to choose who you want to
> live with, who you want to love.(25)

One scene is an interpretive dance against a background of commentators--parents, teacher, psychiatrist
and policeman--who explain how the woman dancer fails to
meet their expectations. Another scene employs mime--a

puppeteer and two "puppets"--to demonstrate manipulation, while still another parodies a television commercial advertising a feminine hygiene deodorant product.

The revue form permits the actors to deal with a broad sampling of feminist issues in an equally broad range of forms. While some scenes, especially the rape scene, seem too didactic, others are quite humorous, and the songs and dances make the production generally entertaining.

An interesting structural device of the play entails an actress' halting the action by saying "stop," whereupon she may freeze the action to comment on the present or upcoming scene. Likewise she calls out "go" to begin the play again. The pauses are scripted, not spontaneous, and in a Brechtian manner provide opportunities for comments on the action and clarification of political points.

Sexpot Follies, the collective's first try at play creation, is an example of the overtness in early feminist work noticed by Judy Chicago and present in so many young groups. Nancy Sugarman said that many of the feminist plays she has read by new groups have scenes almost identical to some in Sexpot Follies.(26) Thus new groups not only tend to be overt, but they often deal with the same issues of feminism. According to Micki Massimino:

> Anger was a driving force behind our first play. ... We didn't write a play about women, we wrote a satire about our anger toward men. We had fallen into a trap common to women's groups, the trap of reaction to men. While it is important to acknowledge the anger in that reaction, it is more important to work beyond it, so the group is free to explore experiences special to women working together.(27)

Circle of the Witch's second play, Lady in the Corner, did move away from cliché, satire and slogans toward an exploration of women's relationships, focusing on a mother, Rachel, and her two daughters, Jenny and Stephanie, in various stages of their lives.

Although the drama is basically realistic, incorporating time lapses between scenes, it begins with a mime of the birth, growth and death of one woman acted out by five actresses. As each stage of development is completed--infancy, childhood, adolescence, adulthood and old age--another actress subtly assumes the persona. The actress of the adulthood stage discovers a wall which blocks her way; she succeeds in knocking a small hole in it and leaves the work for an even older version of herself. The old woman continues the work, tires, surveys her small contribution and dies. This mime, a symbolic repre-

sentation of the whole play, is repeated at the end of the
play.

Utilizing the mother-daughter relationship, the plot
examines childhood fantasies, adolescent expectations,
marriage, divorce, working experiences and male-female
relationships. As the women mature and grow together
they discover that they do have power and must work to
change a society that has encouraged false dreams, goals
and roles.

One particularly well-conceived scene occurs as Jenny
is trying on a wedding dress. A double monologue ensues
as Jenny expresses her doubt about her approaching
wedding, and her mother remembers her own wedding. As
the monologues overlap, Jenny's dressing is mirrored by a
white-masked actress.

The mime scenes are perhaps the play's most interesting. As the play moves through time toward the present, it becomes less dramatic. The last quarter focuses
heavily on the exploitation of working women, and while
the situations portrayed are true and need to be explored
in drama, the play drags because the characters at moments seem mere vehicles for the message.

Clearly Lady in the Corner represents growth in the
collaborative playwriting skills of the Circle of the Witch,
as it tells a complex story through several reasonably
well-developed characters and successfully combines realism
with abstraction in form. The play deals with how women
relate to one another rather than laying blame for women's
oppression as Sexpot Follies did. Like Sexpot Follies,
however, the drama attempts to examine too many issues
for one short play.

Each scene builds around a dominant issue, but the
whole play has no central climax. The dramatic conflict is
resolved as the women move closer together bit by bit and
attain new awareness about life and each other. Nancy
Sugarman said, "Lady in the Corner concerns marriage,
divorce, strikes, etc., but these things are not shown.
Rather we showed the transitions before and after; we
wanted to show how these moments or climaxes
occurred."(28)

Time Is Passing, the story of Minnesota women at the
turn of the century, was Circle of the Witch's contribution
to the Bicentennial and was intended to be a short piece to
tide the group over until it could produce a more significant work. However, the play grew, went through several
revisions and a year later was still being performed.(29)
The theatre group made plans for an audio-slide show of
Time Is Passing for use in schools before retiring the
production.

Time Is Passing is an hour-long documentary-drama
which recaptures women's history through vignettes, songs
of the period, mime, slides and reader's theatre. The
collective gathered the material from pictures, journals,
tapes, newspapers, magazines, letters and people who
lived during the period. It reveals working conditions of
city and rural life, union organizing and strikes, suffra-
gists' efforts and the plight of immigrant, Indian and black
women.

The chief strength of the play is in its authenticity.
As the speeches and dialogues, gleaned from a wealth of
women's history, portray what life was like for a Minnesota
woman entering the twentieth century, slides, gathered
from Minnesota's historical societies relating to the topic,
quell any doubt that what is being said is true.

Because it concerns only a brief period of Minnesota
history, the drama does not portray the lives or achieve-
ments of famous American heroines such as Emma Goldman,
Susan B. Anthony, or Sojourner Truth, as have many
feminist history plays. However, inasmuch as it does show
the ordinary woman overcoming obstacles, it provides role
models for the audience.

Because Time Is Passing is a "history play," the
company found it was welcomed where a "feminist play"
might not be. Much like groups such as New York's
Off-Center Theatre that advocate "sugarcoated socialism,"(30) Circle of the Witch was able to present feminism
in a history lesson package and perform for conservative
groups and public schools.

The three plays of Circle of the Witch are quite
different in form and content, revealing an absence of any
group style. Together they show a political trend from
angry, anti-male and anti-establishment propaganda aimed
at stirring the audience to action, to intimate examinations
of women's lives which act as a consciousness-raiser for
the audience, to a portrayal of women's past which compels
the audience to rediscover their own foremothers and past.

As were similar groups, Circle of the Witch was
experimental. This status, implicit in all feminist art,
means a constant search for new expression and improve-
ments in their art whether or not audiences were satisfied
with preceding attempts.

Circle of the Witch's audiences were predominantly
white, middle or working class, aged 20 to 40. Nancy
Sugarman estimates that over half of the people attending
a community performance were feminists. However, the
company reached out to other audiences. It frequently
performed in schools where it had access to a younger and
hence more politically impressionable audience. Sugarman

commented, "Students rarely have any definite political position, and while sometimes more difficult to perform for than the feminist audiences, students are very important to reach."(31)

The collective sought non-theatregoers and working-class people by performing in parks and neighborhoods, but was only marginally successful in cultivating this audience. Through its regular run of each play coupled with performances throughout the state and the Midwest, Circle of the Witch performed for over 5000 people each year of its existence.

Audience feedback was very important to the collective's work and it devised several ways of obtaining it. Most important was the post-performance discussion. Nancy Sugarman described the process:

> Before the show we introduce ourselves and tell the audience a discussion will follow the play. We always have a discussion leader who asks questions and gets things started. Our note taker records the discussion, and these notes form the basis for changes in the play. Often people want to talk to us individually so we allow time for these exchanges before the group discussion.(32)

The theatre worked with a Community Advisory Board, made up of representatives from different segments of the Twin Cities community, which met with the collective several times a year to give criticism and suggestions.(33)

The last innovation to establish audience contact was the group's newsletter, which detailed the inner workings of the theatre, announced upcoming events and performances and solicited community advice and support. Circulated on the basis of a large mailing list, the newsletter also reached people and theatres outside Minneapolis.

Audience discussion was the chief source of criticism and according to the group, the only one it took seriously. Joyce Indelicato said:

> Reviews are important if that is the only way some people will learn about us. For example, Twin Cities Woman wanted to do an article on us, and even though their readership is not our audience, we granted the interview.(34)

Press reviews were mixed, but few attempted any political analysis of the theatre's work. One interesting review of Sexpot Follies said:

> "Sexpot Follies" was a balance between humor and drama, bringing out various situations that are not funny, which have been laughed at over the ages. It was a successful attempt at com-

bining feminism, art, theatre and politics to point
out the need for change in the country's attitude
toward women, and their role in society.

The pacing and changing of the various skits
were performed with continuity, flowing from one
to another very nicely. They were performed by
some fairly plain, slightly overweight group of
women who did not rely on heavy make-up for
appeal. They came across as ordinary people
stressing a need for change in women's reality
which was well appreciated by the audience.(35)

The reviewer's comment on the actresses' appearance in an
otherwise objective review came under fire by a number of
people who wrote to the newspaper. One letter said:

Such an assinine description is in complete
contrast to the group's satirical assertion that a
woman's physical beauty is of superficial value
only. (A recent review of Dana Talley's recital
performance neglected to mention that he was a
chubby baritone.) The subsequent statement
reads, "They came across as ordinary people...."
Just what was expected?--a group of hysterical,
radical, lesbian activists?(36)

The Minneapolis Star said that Lady in the Corner
was a moderately successful production.

The play is no mere harangue. It seeks to
dramatize its themes, rather than simply illustrate
them with motion; and its characters, although
thinly developed, are at any rate individuals with
identifiable personalities.

"Lady in the Corner" is predictably uneven--too
many authors invariably weaken a play--but the
members of Circle of the Witch are giving it an
energetic, unpolished presentation.(37)

Another review, indicating growth in perception and playwriting skills, contrasted this play with Sexpot Follies.

Although the message is obvious, it's a lot less
strident than Circle of the Witch's first production, Sexpot Follies.... Lady in the Corner is
the kind of play one older woman liked because
"it isn't so dreadfully feminist."(38)

Common Ground faulted the play's failure to portray the
personal transformation of the characters, but it praised
the bridal shop scene and the factory worker scene.

The second powerful scene was the "mechanical
ballet" done by Jenifer and the workers on their
way to the factory. Donning white masks, the
entire group turns into factory equipment.(39)

The company's history drama, Time Is Passing, received a favorable notice from a St. Paul newspaper.

> [I]t was an informative, emotional, and inoffen-
> sive play. It entertained, and although the
> performance time was short, it did a remarkable
> job in attempting to educate and increase aware-
> ness in our surroundings.(40)

A reviewer from Augsburg College, however, found the
production "adequate," the acting "decent" and felt more
compelled to watch the slides than the acting.(41) While
the collective realized it needed to improve, it rated its
own work well above average. As Nancy Sugarman put it,
"We're probably a B+."(42)

The group noticed that male audience criticism was
directly related to the degree of acceptance of feminism by
men.

> One man said that "this propaganda doesn't relate
> to me; I can't identify with it and it's boring."
> But most criticism is positive. In Time Is Passing
> men said that they now realized what they had
> missed because history has come only through the
> male point of view.(43)

Unlike the A & T, which usually focused on specific
Minneapolis political issues, Circle of the Witch dealt with
more theoretical questions and thus measuring its success
is more difficult. However, indicators such as growth in
audience and membership, receipt of grants and increased
accessibility pointed to some success. Audience feedback
in the form of personal letters shows that the theatre was
affecting its audience. Writing about Lady in the Corner,
one woman said, "If all women and men could have been as
touched and moved as I was watching 'Lady,' human liberation would not be quite as hard."(44) After a performance of Time Is Passing at a Chaska, Minnesota, high
school, the theatre received the following comment:

> Both the kids and the staff have highly compli-
> mented the performance and the performers....
> I'd just like to add that the play has indeed
> provoked some of the kids into searching out
> some old family stories and history.(45)

About the same play presented at the Park Avenue Senior
Citizens Center, someone wrote:

> Your play was meaningful and very well pre-
> sented. It seems remarkable how you, being so
> young, can interpret so exactly and with such
> sensitivity, the dilemma of women in "the olden
> days," long before you were even born.(46)

In terms of its stated goals, the theatre group suc-
ceeded. When one considers the time and energy spent by

the members for almost no pay, the extended existence of
the group is amazing. Believing that the woman's experience is different from the man's and that this experience
needs to be reflected in art, the collective saw feminist
theatre as a viable art for some time to come.(47)

In four years, Circle of the Witch went from an
almost anti-male position to a pro-woman one as reflected
in its drama and collective discussion notes.(48) Its later
plays encouraged consciousness-raising and individual
action but abandoned inciting audience group action as it
did in its first one. The artistic quality rose over the
years. Nancy Sugarman commented:

> We've grown in four years, and our plays have
> become less overt. We've been able to work more
> on style and form than on content and to explore
> new methods. However, this process also means
> that it is more difficult now to incorporate women
> without theatre experience into the group.(49)

In the spring of 1977, Circle of the Witch incorporated
three new women into the collective. All had some theatre
training and two were from racial minorities. Its fourth
play, The Changebringers, A Fantasy of Women and Work,
opened October 7, 1977, at the Firehouse Theatre in
Minneapolis.(50)

Chapter V

AT THE FOOT OF THE MOUNTAIN

Minneapolis' newest feminist theatre, At the Foot of
the Mountain, was formed in the spring of 1974 by a group
of three male and three female actors.   After its first two
productions it went into an inactive transition period.   Jan
Magrane and Martha Boesing rekindled interest in the
theatre, and in 1976, the group reemerged as an all-female
feminist theatre collective.

Like most other feminist theatres, members are white
and middle class, but unlike most groups, members are
older, ranging in age from mid-twenties to mid-forties.
All have extensive experience and education in theatre.
Martha Boesing has an M.A. in English literature, was a
core member of the Firehouse Theatre and co-founder of
the Minneapolis Repertory Theatre and the Moppet Players,
and has published over a dozen plays.   Anne Bowman has
taught acting in Minneapolis schools, was a founder of the
Alive and Trucking Theatre and is completing a degree in
women's studies.   Jam Magrane has a B.A. in acting and
directing, was a resident at Atlanta's Academy Theatre for
three years, and teaches acting.   Miriam Monasch has a
B.A. in theatre, was a founder of the Grinell Mime Troupe,
and is a song writer.   Robyn Samuels has a B.A. in
theatre and an M.F.A. in directing and teaches creative
dramatics.   Phyllis Jane Wagner has a Ph.D. in theatre,
worked with several experiemental theatres in Colorado and
Maine, and for three years was assistant professor and
chairperson of Southern Illinois University's directing
program.(1)   In addition to their wide and varied academic
and practical experience, individuals continue to take
theatre courses, and the entire company studies Kristin
Linklater's vocal training method and Mabel Dodd's movement exercises.(2)

The members' credentials have bearing on the high
quality of their work but make recruitment of new members
difficult.   The membership has remained stable in the past
year, but the company says it would like to have women

from minority backgrounds join it. However, such women
must be feminist, have some theatre experience or skill
approaching the group's level and be able to work with the
collective approximately 40 hours a week.(3)

Although the group had one of the male former members of the company perform with it in its production of
The Moon Tree, it chose to remain a separatist group.
Martha Boesing says, "at this point it is important that the
collective be just women because we give away our power
to men."(4)

In a 1976 brochure, At the Foot of the Mountain
stated its philosophy as follows:

> At the Foot of the Mountain is a women's theatre--
> emergent, stuggling, angry, joyous. Through our
> own consciousness-raising, workshops in vocal and
> body awareness, and varied improvisational and
> Gestalt disciplines, we are now in the process of
> developing a company voice, a company style. We
> are asking: What is a woman's space? What is a
> women's ritual? How does it differ from the theatre
> of the patriarchy? We struggle to relinquish trad-
> itions such as linear plays, proscenium theatre,
> non-participatory ritual and seek to reveal theatre
> that is circular, intuitive, personal, involving. We
> are a theatre of protest, witnesses to the destruc-
> tiveness of a society which is alienated from itself,
> and a theatre of celebration, participants in the
> prophesy of a new world which is emerging through
> the rebirth of women's consciousness.

This description emphasizes the emergent state of the
feminist theatre and its turning away from a focus on
product. "The big thing about our theatre is that we're
process oriented. By definition we try to look at what is
going on, try to identify it, and let that be the work."(5)

Believing that most feminist theatre in America today
is actually women-oriented theatre within the bounds of the
patriarchy, At the Foot of the Mountain is seeking to
invent feminist or matriarchal theatre. Matriarchy does
not imply a role reversal within the current political system but is centered on the collective distribution of power,
the abuse of which the group believes is the key issue in
patriarchy.

Implicit in the group's theory of feminism as a revolutionary movement is the representation of female qualities
which have been denigrated throughout history. Martha
Boesing says that such "female" qualities as intuition,
emotion, nurturing, healing and supporting must be owned
and developed by women, not repressed and substituted for
by "male" qualities of powerfulness, analysis, aggression
and competition.(6)

In a workshop on the theatre of the patriarch versus feminist theatre, At the Foot of the Mountain uses the following chart to demonstrate the differences.

MALE Patriarchal Values	FEMALE Matriarchal Values
Product	Process
Individualistic	Collective
Hierarchical	Mutual
Analytical	Emotional
Set	Emergent
Codified	Changing
Logical	Intuitive
Linear	Cyclical
Competitive	Supportive
Abstract ideas	Concrete images, details
Rigid	Fluid
Conservative	Radical
Reactionary	Revolutionary
Normal	Deviant
Single-minded	Suffused
Ejaculatory	Multi-orgasmic
Answers	Questions (7)

At the Foot of the Mountain is attempting to develop these female traits through its work.

The audience, structure and methods of the collective reflect its search for a feminist theatre. Members of At the Foot of the Mountain's audiences are predominantly white females, aged 20 to 40 who are not theatregoers. Phyllis Wagner says that the theatre gets audiences as large as any Minneapolis fringe theatre, averaging eighty persons per performance. With eighteen performances of three shows a year plus tours, At the Foot of the Mountain performs for over 5000 people yearly.(8)

Feminists, including the lesbian community, are major supporters of the theatre. Boesing comments:

The support the theatre has gotten from the women's movement is enormous. They've really allowed us to be their theatre and cultural voice. Ten years ago we wouldn't have been regarded with this kind of esteem and respect; it wouldn't have been possible to create this kind of theatre then.(9)

Since a matriarch embraces males too, the theatre encourages men to attend its performances, although it admits that right now its work will necessarily speak more to women.(10)

Unlike the A & T and Circle of the Witch, At the Foot of the Mountain does not perform guerrilla and agitprop pieces or attempt to bring its theatre to the people by performing in neighborhoods. It performs mostly in accessible small theatres such as the Pillsbury-Waite Cultural Arts Center, Theatre 1900 or the Walker Church, for low admission prices, but members say that are more interested in art which is political than in the theatrical politics of agitprop and street theatre. However, this potentially elitist position concerns the company. "The problem with not doing agitprop and working for art and a new style is the danger of becoming esoteric, a theatre for a small group of sophisticated women and not really a people's theatre."(11)

Methods to contact and involve audiences outside performances include mailing brochures and newsletters, holding open workshops, encouraging discussions after performances and at special community response sessions, and inviting the community to view and criticize works-in-progress.(12)

In the fall of 1979 the active staff consisted of nine women who share all artistic, technical and administrative theatre work.

We find it important within the collective structure, which is leaderless, to name the "leaders" who are in fact operating. Rita Mae Brown talks about having a collective task figure who identifies the task or path. There can also be a maintenance leader, etc.(13)

Martha Boesing and Phyllis Wagner are called co-directors of the company and Wagner serves as the touring manager.

The theatre, which operates on a professional, fulltime basis with no members employed fulltime elsewhere, manages to support its members with money from grants, workshops and performance earnings and donations. Grants from sources such as the National Endowment for the Arts and the Minnesota Arts Council have totaled less than $7000, and admission prices of $3 per person and touring fees of $1000 per performance have hardly made the company solvent. The theatre pays each member a salary of about $300 a month and, because it pays unemployment insurance, during part of the year members collect unemployment benefits. Members have been willing to adjust their lifestyles to their low incomes in order to work with their theatre fulltime. While the group has in part solved the time-and-money problem which fractures and distracts all small, poor theatres, it would like to be able to retreat for a year to devote the more intense work with the development of a feminist theatre that performance obligations have so far prohibited.(14)

At the Foot of the Mountain is the resident theatre at the Pillsbury-Waite Cultural Arts Center where it rents rehearsal space and works four hours each morning. Another twenty to thirty hours weekly is spent in performing and attending to theatre business.(15)

The collective has worked in three modes: producing a scripted play such as Megan Terry's Babes in the Bighouse, creating a group-written piece such as The Story of a Mother and producing group-playwright collaborations such as The Moon Tree in which member Martha Boesing developed a script with the help of the company. The group prefers collaborative works because it has had trouble with the content of most outside scripts. However, members indicate that if they found a suitable script they would produce it because, first, it would be easy as compared with creating their own, and second, they see a danger of becoming too ingrown if they do only their own plays.(16)

So far the company has produced: Pimp, The Gelding,   River Journal,   Raped: A Woman's Look at Brecht's Exception and the Rule, Love Song for an Amazon, Babes in the Bighouse and The Moon Tree. The Story of a Mother opened in Minneapolis in March 1978. After a six-week run, shows are toured until the opening of a new play. Raped, however, has been kept as a touring piece and was reworked in September 1977 for further tours.

At the Foot of the Mountain is a group of highly skilled and experienced theatre artists. Besides possessing acting and directing talents some members have worked in various types of psychological therapy and have transposed this experience into theatre exercises. A Gestalt therapist works with the group to facilitate this experimentation.(17) Phyllis Wagner comments:

> I think the most important work we've done has been feeling work, exercises that were therapy but have now become acting tools. They have to do with the skill of preparation rather than the skill of moving, singing, etc. They are internal tools for the actor. We're trying to discover a new acting technique in which we can use our feelings of the moment.(18)

Martha Boesing continues:

> We come to the rehearsal time from a woman's space, springing out of those parts of ourselves which have traditionally belonged to women: our feelings, our intuitions, our hysteria (hystera: womb). It is a terrifying leap we make. We have always been told to leave our feelings at the door,

mask the sorrow, anxiety, even the joy, approach
our work with objectivity and clarity. We start
with awareness.... As we go through the script,
we try to keep in contact with our own internal
processes and let them be our guide, let them
direct the moment. We avoid analyzing the feelings
of the character, avoid objective delineation of
personality, avoid setting the moment.

We are heading towards an improvisational theatre
event. There is the script, there are the same
people, with the same names and the same actions
each night, but the emotional life changes from
moment to moment, performance to performance, and
the texture of the play, the subtext, is totally new
each time the performers come to it.... We have
just begun to scratch the surface of what it means
to relinquish our minds, our knowledge, our objective control of the environment to our feelings, our
intuitions.(19)

Psychological work extends to ingroup operation as
members insist on open communication and have developed
means to insure it. "We sit and share our feelings every
day and confront everything. We stay clear with each
other. If it means dragging down the rehearsal and the
'work' doesn't get done, we go with that; that becomes the
work."(20)

This method is obviously at variance with that of
traditional theatres which must get the show on. However,
At the Foot of the Mountain seems to have discovered a
method for group dynamics that may ultimately save it time
and will certainly be reflected in performance. For example, if a rehearsal is boring or going badly, the company does not force itself to feign a show of energy.
Rather, members discuss why the process is boring, work
through exercises related to the problem and let that work
become the rehearsal. Thus members are able to bring
their immediate feelings to their work and dispense with
counter-productive means. This method best explains what
the group means by being process oriented.

Not all of the theatre's work involves deep psychological investigation. In its playwright-collective creations
it has utilized improvisation. One member notes the process used in writing The Moon Tree.

Martha conceived the idea for the play over two
years ago, wrote the roles of the wives with the
women in the acting company in mind, and finished
the complete script in August.... When we came
back to The Moon Tree seven months later Martha
did not bring the script; instead she reminded the

cast of the plot, gave each actor a character sketch, and asked us to improvise the whole play. Every day for the next two weeks she spent time exploring the cores of the characters and the cores of their madnesses improvisationally. Martha then rewrote the script from rehearsal discoveries and this on-going exchange between actors and play-wright is how The Moon Tree was created.(21)

At the Foot of the Mountain does not yet perceive a company style in its work: Phyllis Wagner says, "We haven't spent enough time together so that the content is really organic."(22) Because the group has mostly done plays by Martha Boesing, who does have a writing style, a performance, if not an acting, style is perceptible in the company. Boesing's plays, while all quite different, are all non-linear, non-realistic, Brechtian and multi-layered, springing from an emotional dynamic usually between a male and a female. The following explications of River Journal and The Moon Tree will explain the ideas and style the company presents through its member-playwright.

River Journal is a women's ritual employing symbolic events and images and Brechtian epic theatre devices. The story centers on Ann, an allegorical Everywoman, who learns in the process of the play to cast off her masks and look inside herself. The play begins with a ritual, the wedding of Ann and Myles, overseen by Snake, a priestess or mother-goddess figure who follows, comments on and encourages Ann's development. Snake announces each of the 17 scene titles; Scene Two is called "Myles Is Intro-duced to Vera and Carla and the Intrigue Begins."(23) Vera and Carla are Ann's two sisters who live with her and at the same time are different facets of Ann herself. Vera, who wears a courtesan mask, is the sensuous man-pleasing side of Ann, and Carla, represented by an old crone mask, is the nurturer who takes care of things and keeps peace. The sisters' wedding presents to Ann are the masks.

As the relationship of Myles and Ann continues, Ann become more disillusioned and her increasing hysteria is revealed through excerpts from her journal which get more and more bizarre as the play goes on.

Summoning up her rage and the violent fantasies she has secretly recorded in her journal, Ann gains the strength to face her madness and ends up in a solitary, ambiguous position, resolved to continue but lacking direction.(24)

The play ends as it began, in ceremony, with Ann leaving her husband and her past as she ritualistically

burns the whore and the mother masks then sings with the
cast.

> The die is cast
> The dead no longer singing.
> What's done is done
> The pendulum is swinging.
>> The question is laid out
>> For each of us to ask,
>> Whether to hold on
>> Or to drop the mask [p. 60].(25)

The uncertainty of what the protagonist will do was
criticized by one feminist publication. "Regardless of the
rebirth symbolism, River Journal deals primarily with
destruction. What about the grave problems the independent woman faces? Ann may no longer be lost, but her
road is treacherous."(26) The reviewer's desire for answers and perhaps role models is understandable. Although the play's tone is optimistic, the author opted for
revealing a single rite of passage based on her own feelings about the lack of answers rather than projecting
solutions. The critic's discontent stems from an awareness
that since Nora slammed the door, most feminist drama has
dwelt on presenting the problem. There have been some
answers since Ibsen, and the critic's desire to see them
should be considered by feminist theatres and playwrights.

In typical Brechtian manner each main point in River
Journal is demonstrated by a song. The "Author's Notes"
suggest that the music is reminiscent of folk ballads,
spirituals, blues or madrigals, "that kind of nostalgic
sense of longing." A reviewer added, "The numerous rich
musical interludes and background--chanting, plainsong,
rounds--form an intricate sound sculpture."(27) There
are 17 songs in River Journal, including a few verse repe-
titions. Especially exciting is Snake's song in which she
tells Ann and the audience who she is. The third verse
says:

> In an age of mass oppression
> And severely felt repression,
> There is limited indiscretion,
> And the merest dark suggestion
> Can give you indiges-tion! [p. 3].

One particularly beautiful song is the Demeter song which
Ann's mother (actually the ghost of her mother) sings to
her as she struggles with her insanity.

The themes of madness, power manipulation and
awakening consciousness are closely associated with male-
female relationships: primarily, that of Ann and Myles,
and secondarily, Ann and her father. The men, while

responsible in part for Ann's predicament, are sympathetically portrayed as products of their socialization. The
chorus of Dad's song says:
>   What is a man to do?
>   Misguided and misinformed,
>   He throws himself on the waters of life,
>   And surrenders himself to the storm [p. 33].

"It is implicit that they must make the leap from acknow-
ledgement of their failings to some sort of positive change,
however."(28)

Hysteria and madness, themes repeated in The Moon
Tree, are viewed by the playwright as positive sources of
knowledge, not as sources of fear. In a newspaper article
Martha Boesing said:
>   Recently I've been into claiming all the things that
>   are seen as "feminine" and bad in myself. We are
>   trained to see our so-called evil, witchy, hysterical
>   aspects as negative because they are associated
>   with women. But I've really started to see them as
>   positive. I think we have to claim all the sup-
>   posedly evil parts of women and be them in order
>   to get unstuck.(29)

The Moon Tree, which according to its author is still
in progress, exposes the lunacy of women who, locked into
a male world, are misunderstood and deemed crazy. The
play fluctuates not between reality and illusion, but between reality and a more real fantasy. The entire theatre
becomes an insane asylum; at one side is a stage or platform with a study/living-room set. Men in the audience
are seated and assume the roles of asylum visitors; the
women are all inmates and may wander about, sitting
anywhere. The action begins as the asylum nurse announces the characters and setting.

In her introduction to the play Martha Boesing says:
>   This play is about three women who have been
>   committed to an insane asylum. They were all
>   married, at different times, to the same man, a
>   well-known writer. They each believe themselves to
>   be mad and at fault for the tragic ending to their
>   marriage. They are fortunate enough to be put in
>   the care of a loving nurse who realizes that by
>   reexposing themselves to their own pain and anger
>   they will heal themselves and pass through madness
>   into another consciousness. To help this healing
>   come about, the nurse invites their husband and
>   his current wife to act out their life as it is now,
>   in the form of a short play to be presented at the
>   asylum for the three wives to attend. The husband
>   agrees to this, believing it just might be the jab

> his soul needs to get him writing again. His cur-
> rent wife goes along, led by her curiosity. What
> follows from this event is a journey through lunacy,
> back home.(30)

The three wives are all crazy and their husband, Schooner,
has made them that way given the present social system.
However, the women's madness is shown to be a result of
some collusion between Schooner and his wives. Schooner
prospers at their expense, but the women also participate
in the charade.

The roles that women play, as more obviously drawn
in River Journal, are revealed through the former wives,
Eel, Fish Bones and Leviathan and the current wife,
Crustacea, all possessing characteristics associated with
their sea-creature names.

The dramatic action, often simultaneous, flashes back
and forth from the story on the platform acted out in a
formal, realistic, "Pinter" style to that in the asylum--the
whole theatre. Sound and movement create the strange
atmosphere as the actresses hiss, squeal, dance, gestic-
ulate, form statues and sing childhood rhymes to articulate
their pain, bare their souls and begin to understand
themselves and each other.

The fourth wife, Crustacea, is successfully lured by
the former wives and, joining them, comes to understand
as they have the nature of woman's lunacy. As Crustacea
leaves Schooner for the asylum he says:

Schooner: You don't hate me, do you Crustacea?

Crustacea: Nope.

Schooner: We had some good times together.

Crustacea: Yep.

Schooner: What will I do now?

Crustacea: Do! Same thing you've always done.
            Have yourself a good shit and write a
            new book.

Schooner: No secrets, no secrets left in the old
            man. They're all looney in there you
            know.

Crustacea: All depends on how you look at it, I
            guess. Good-bye Schooner [p. 58].

As Schooner digs into writing his book, Fish Bones
with all the asylum women tells a fable about a tribe of
women who came together under the moon tree.

And the women came from all around. And they
opened their arms and they sat together under the
moon tree and they embraced their lunacy and they
shared their stories--each and everyone, until they
were finished. And it was quiet....
    And they never forgot what the old woman said:
"Only by sharing all of your stories will you become
empty. And only when you are empty can you be
filled" [pp. 59-60].
Eel tells the audience that they may leave, or they may
stay and sit under the moon tree.
    Audience members who stayed shared their feelings
with the performers, and although the drama was discussed, it was not an intellectual analysis, but an emotional sharing of stories and lives. Since from entering
the theatre the women had been asked to claim their own
madness, the audience participation was not strained or
manipulative. The discussion became an integral part of
the play, a semi-religious or ritualistic communal experience.
    The theme of women and madness, the subject of
much recent literature and films such as Diary of a Mad
Housewife, Three Women and Woman Under the Influence,
is handled by At the Foot of the Mountain in a manner of
controlled insanity. One does not see a realistic day-by-
day crumbling of a woman due to the role she is forced to
play in society. Rather one experiences a multi-layered or
mosaic rendering of madness which shifts in time and place
reminiscent of dreams. The madness permeates the whole
theatre; all the women, audience and performers, are
crazy, and the men are perpetrators and witnesses.
    The Moon Tree, however, is not anti-male, although
it was perceived by some people as such. Boesing says
she created Schooner with much love and understanding.
While he is responsible for his behavior, he is also a product of a sexist society.(31) Boesing is saying that we all
have to change.
    River Journal and The Moon Tree are thematically
similar but theatrically different. The crisp, Brechtian
River Journal with realistic scenes, readings, songs and
characters so stripped down they are most like one aspect
of single personality, contrasts with The Moon Tree's
emotional pull, time, space and place shifts and audience
involvement. River Journal is more didactic and uses
ceremonious ritual; The Moon Tree is more subtle and
rather than showing ritual, precipitates it in the theatre
with the audience as participants. Both plays bear the
mark of an experienced playwright familiar not only with
language but with the theatre. As products of a writer's

well-defined vision, the plays appear neither arty nor
phoney.

According to the collective, audiences have been
extremely enthusiastic about its work.(32) Media criticism,
less important to the group, has also been good, frequently commenting on the ensemble's acting skill. "The acting
is really superb and is what carries off the multi-faceted
messages."(33) "Much of the play's [River Journal] ability
to elicit a response is due to the fine ensemble work of the
cast, sensitively directed by Boesing."(34) "Like most of
Ms. Boesing's previous collaborations ... Raped is an
occasionally outrageous, consistently thought-provoking
evening of highly political theatre."(35) Of Raped, the
Village Voice said:

> I find the work of At the Foot of the Mountain to
> be first rate. To begin with Miriam Monasch, one of
> the performers, has written a fine, crisp new
> adaptation of the play. And the physical work of
> the performers is a joy. They are deftly guided by
> director Phyllis Jane Wagner and are agile and
> precise as they stalk, pounce, bend, sway. And
> they are compelling musically.... The group is
> easily one of the best disciplined ensembles I have
> encountered....(36)

Males, a minority in most At the Foot of the Mountain
audiences, respond less often and not as deeply to performances. "Women generally see themselves and men say the
play is too personal or that they don't understand or are
confused. With Raped, the men there were sure we were
not talking about them."(37) However, critic Arthur
Sainer had this to say about his experience at Raped:

> As a male, what the play brought home to me more
> starkly than ever before is the sense that women
> must feel they are living in an armed camp, that
> they are the Niggers of Sex. It is one thing for a
> male to feel pained at the sight of a woman being
> ogled as she walks down the street; it is quite
> another to be that woman 24 hours a day--on the
> street, in subways, on the job, in her own
> home.(38)

It is difficult to measure the success of At the Foot
of the Mountain because its members reject most traditional
success indicators. When invited to perform at the pres-
tigious Alternative Theatre Festival in 1977, they declined
because they suspected they would be a hit and that this
kind of success would inhibit the work they want to do.
However, reviews have been favorable, membership has
been stable, audiences have grown and grants have increased.

The theatre's own measure of success relates to its continued discovery of what a women's theatre could be.

> We strive to create theatre that is informed by consciousness rather than rhetoric, to move audiences rather than chastise them, and to be as committed to understanding the theatre as we are to understanding human liberation.(39)

One step toward its goal, as begun with The Moon Tree and expanded in the Equinox and Hallowmass celebrations, involves performing not plays, but participatory rituals capable of fostering change in people's lives. The group sees the shamanistic possibilities of the theatre artist and how theatre can be a cathartic and healing experience for the audience. As they develop techniques which will ultimately result in such ritual performances, they continue to create from personal experiences to arrive at universal meanings.(40)

Chapter VI

COMPARISONS AND CONTRASTS

Theatre history reveals that social and political plays have been performed since antiquity. During times of intense political activity such theatre has flourished, and in the 20th century in the United States the 1930's and the 1960's constitute two such periods, the former initiated by the Great Depression and the latter by the Vietnam War and civil rights controversies.

Feminist theatre activity is comparable to the political theatre activity of these two periods. It is useful first to contrast the four Minneapolis feminist theatre groups, and then to compare feminist theatre of the 1970's, as represented by the Minneapolis groups, with political theatre of the 1930's, specifically the Communist Party theatres and the Federal Theatre, and with political theatre of the 1960's, specifically blacks'.

The outstanding characteristic of feminist theatres in Minneapolis has been their use of collective organization. All four groups used this method because it avoids hierarchies and competition for position and it promotes sharing of skills and responsibilities.

In theatre, however, the communal handling of power can be a problem since in any group certain individuals may be more talanted or skilled than others. The system has the potential for creating low artistic quality in performances, but this has not happened in the Minneapolis groups for several reasons. First, feminist theatre groups are small, averaging seven members, each member having the opportunity to be heard, with individual talents contributing to the best group advantage. Second, collectivity does not mean that any individual can demand a particular role or job just because there is no central authority. Rather, task assignments are decided upon by group discussion and decision. The system takes more time than that used by a group based on a hierarchical structure, but it works well in small groups dedicated to a single ideology. The process has a more spiritual base

79

than establishment theatre permits and is perhaps only
possible because the groups are such close-knit organizations. Thus collectivity entails a sense of responsibility to
the group and because members have equal power, groups
ultimately have more artisitic freedom.

While collective organization is a hallmark of feminist
theatre, all groups do not employ it in the same way. The
Alive and Trucking group set up ad hoc committees for
various duties and needs; Circle of the Witch assigned
tasks to individuals and rotated duties; the Lavender
Cellar had no standing committees or tasks but worked
from production to production encouraging flexibility in
work assignments; and At the Foot of the Mountain tried
to recognize abilities within the group without designating
leaders.

The Lavender Cellar was able to use the Lesbian
Resource Center for business purposes since its needs
were not great; the other groups each selected and paid a
member to act as a business manager for a period of time.
Only At the Foot of the Mountain paid all members salaries.
The Lavender Cellar members received no remuneration and
the A & T and Circle of the Witch members received token
fees and reimbursements for wages lost in order to perform.

The four groups have utilized collectivity to meet
their particular needs. The structure is used as a guiding
philosophy, not as a rigid method, and thus changes as
the needs of the group change.

Besides being organized collectively, these four
Minneapolis groups also commonly have lacked money.
Although the 1975 budget for the A & T was ten times that
of the Lavender Cellar, when it was spread over the
number of performances, budgets were comparable. Groups
did not raise ticket prices because this would have meant
that poorer people could not attend shows. Instead, there
was a trend toward increased grant seeking to alleviate
financial problems and as the groups matured they learned
how to apply for and get more grants. More money,
however, would not have meant lavish productions since
these companies were not interested in Broadway opulence.
Increased funds would permit groups to pay salaries to
members and, perhaps, to operate fulltime.

Another common denominator among groups is the
tremendous amount of time spent by members in theatre
activities. At the Foot of the Mountain has spent the most
time in theatre work mainly because it works fulltime and
its members have more radically altered their lifestyles to
work at the theatre. Its forty-hour week is followed in
order of time expended by Circle of the Witch, the A & T

and the Lavender Cellar. Time expenditures, however, relate to the amount of activity or production methods and are not valid measures of group commitment. That each member of each group was dedicated to her theatre appears obvious.

While individual members' political backgrounds and beliefs have been impossible to assess, artistic backgrounds have been shown to be varied. Both the A & T and the Lavender Cellar members had little theatre training. The A & T was making progress in artistic improvement when it broke up; the Lavender Cellar became inactive before it was able to do so. Circle of the Witch did not require members to have previous theatre experience although most had some; At the Foot of the Mountain members were all trained and desired that new members be similarly experienced. Naturally, the members' theatre backgrounds will influence what the theatres attempt. However, each group seems to have developed a way to utilize effectively the talents of members and has done well whatever its particular forte.

The A & T found success in social satire and musical comedy which best exhibited its members' talents. The Lavender Cellar used the revue form to promote individual contributions and realistic drama to use its member-playwright's talents. Circle of the Witch's plays have been quite different--satirical revue, realistic drama and documentary--but each has allowed the actor-writers a personal voice in the play through collective playwriting. At the Foot of the Mountain has worked mainly with the plays of its member-playwright which develop and utilize the company's non-realistic, experimental style.

The rhetoric of all four companies has been similar as expressed in programs, pamphlets, articles and brochures: raising consciousnesses, presenting the woman's experience, providing work opportunities in theatre for women, offering an alternative to male-dominated theatre and entertaining. Each group, however, has emphasized different things which have made it slightly different from the others.

The purpose of the Lavender Cellar was to give lesbian-feminist women an opportunity in theatre and to express the gay woman's point of view for lesbians. The A & T's primary goal was to perform socialist-feminist plays for a large audience and to bring that audience to political action. Circle of the Witch has had a specifically feminist orientation and has desired a working-class audience whose consciousness it has sought to raise through the presentation of collectively-written plays. At the Foot of the Mountain is a matriarchal-feminist theatre which has

sought to discover not a woman-oriented theatre within
establishment theate but a completely new feminist theatre.
It is the most experimental theatre of the four and has
tended toward ritual and participatory events for feminists.

All groups believed that all art is political; none
intentionally focused more on art or politics. However,
the work of the A & T and Circle of the Witch has tended
to be more overt or political in a sociological sense while
At the Foot of the Mountain's work is more psychological.
The Lavender Cellar's revues were outright agitprop, but
its play Cory was a psychological drama although less
sophisticated than the plays of At the Foot of the Mountain.

These trends parallel the amount and kind of group
political study-discussion done by each organization. The
A & T and Circle of the Witch held political study sessions
as part of their processes. The Lavender Cellar and At
the Foot of the Mountain had no such sessions but incorporated political discussion into their rehearsal processes.

All groups employed some method to allow members to
voice their personal feelings individually. The A & T used
criticism/self-criticism, Circle of the Witch and At the Foot
of the Mountain conducted special emotional response
sessions, and the Lavender Cellar took time to treat personal issues during rehearsals. These personal discussions became an important aspect of each group's process
and strongly influenced its work.

Feminist theatres say they are process rather than
product oriented, meaning the methods used in the development of a theatre piece are equally as important as the
end result. Traditional establishment theatres are organized on a hierarchical basis which promotes a pecking
order within a company. This method is the most efficient
when the end product is the primary concern. Collective
theatres are equally interested in the process, first because, as permanent companies, members work closely
together for long periods and try to develop new techniques for learning and gaining experience. The acting
ensemble has time to alter and improve productions.
Second, their personal involvement with their companies
and dedication to feminism relate to their valuing the
means to the end. Actually there is no end; the process
is continuous and there is no thought of setting a production.

Part of their process has involved rethinking traditional values of the theatre. Some things were kept;
others were discarded. What is significant is that these
groups were experimenting and testing new concepts and
approaches. Their rejection of traditional criteria for
evaluation and for success is part of this questioning.

Being successful to them does not mean being invited to perform in New York City or at theatre festivals or getting rave reviews. They believe that being successful in most traditional terms inhibits being successful on their own terms. In much the same way that black theatres reject white influence and criticism, feminist theatres reject traditional evaluation. Not only does such criticism usually come from non-feminist males, it usually fails to perceive what is being attempted through performances.

Feminist theatre is still developing, but its methods have freely subsumed those of the radical theatres of the 1960's whenever it has found them suitable. Other methods used in the groups' work processes include a wide assortment of exercises coming from individual member's theatre backgrounds. Those groups with trained and/or experienced members have produced less amateur works, but as stated before, each group managed to develop a method and style in keeping with its abilities.

The relationship between feminist theatres and radical theatres, as explained in Chapter I, was to be expected. It appears, however, that feminist theatres are more successful than were the radical theatres in achieving their goals. For example, collectivity is given much more than lip-service in the feminist groups. The experimental theatres, while more democratic than establishment theatres, had definite leaders. Feminist theatres have no such leaders. Perhaps because members have a dual responsibility, to feminism and to theatre, they seem to be more committed. Feminist theatre's political goals are specific enough to sharpen the political commitment, whereas the vague anti-establishment ideologies of many radical theatres were often less than compelling for members.

In choice of material, Circle of the Witch is the only group that has never used other than a collectively written play. The A & T did The Independent Female and The Exception and the Rule; the Lavender Cellar produced member Pat Suncircle's Prisons and Cory; and At the Foot of the Mountian produced member Martha Boesing's plays, Brecht's The Exception and the Rule and Megan Terry's Babes in the Bighouse. However, most material used by all groups was written either collectively or by a group member. In addition to plays, the A & T and Circle of the Witch have produced numerous agitprop skits and guerrilla theatre pieces.

Since all four groups are poor, technical requirements and embellishments have been kept to a minimum. In the collectively written plays technical necessities were avoided in the script. In other plays the technical possibilities were dictated by a tight budget.

The dominant issue dealt with by the theatres has been gender-role stereotyping. All groups have examined rape in at least one play and have produced women's history plays. Non-realistic forms have dominated these groups' dramas whether in revues, fantasies, skits or documentaries. Only Cory, Lady in the Corner and Battered Homes and Gardens could be considered realistic, and the first two included several non-realistic devices such as mime, while Battered Homes and Gardens is actually a musical comedy.

While all the groups professed a dedication to audience and utilized post-performance discussion and other techniques to get audience feedback, only the Lavender Cellar was competely succesful in getting the audience it sought--a lesbian one. However, its goal was easier to achieve than that of the A & T and Circle of the Witch which sought a broader audience to include those who rarely or never attended the theatre in the past.

The Lavender Cellar was again unique in that it was the only group which excluded men from certain performances and did not attempt to have the audience participate in its productions. The A & T and At the Foot of the Mountain both experimented with sex-segregation of the audience and used various techniques such as audience sing-alongs and the assumption of roles by women in the audience as participation devices. Circle of the Witch encouraged audience involvement through its presentational style in Sexpot Follies and by integrating discussions with the audience into its performances.

The audiences of the four Minneapolis feminist theatres were supportive; their enthusiasm may be interpreted as indicating a need for such a theatre. There has been no competition for audiences among groups, although 1975 was the only year in which all four were performing. This lack of competition, however, is most related to the fact that each group was different and that seeing one did not mean one had seen them all.

Media criticism, with the exception of that of At the Foot of the Mountain, which has always received positive reviews, has generally tended to praise the group's energy and audacity but to note the need for better acting and better plays. Reviewers, however, have consistently ignored the differing objectives of these feminist theatres. Certainly, some critique of each group's political statement as made through its work would be in order, but such analysis has been neglected except by a few feminist publications. Newspaper reviews do not concern the groups because members believe that a traditional point of view is inappropriate for an experimental theatre. Favorable reviews are only valued for their power to bring in a new audience.

Political Theatres of the 1930's

During the 1930's political theatre in America flourished primarily because of increased political awareness stimulated by the economic depression. Communist Party theatres, the Theatre Union, the Labor Stage, the Federal Theatre, the Mercury Theatre, the Theatre Guild, the Group Theatre and even Broadway, together produced quantities of social and political drama.

The Communist Party controlled or had influence over a number of theatres in the United States during the 1930's.

> The Communists believed that the theatre could help foment their revolution against American capitalism and all of its Depression evils. They believed further that the drama would be useful as a propaganda agency in the period of reconstruction when the Party would lead the country forward first to the proletarian state and then to the classless society.(1)

The earliest communist groups produced short agitprop skits. Agitprops were inexpensive and easy to produce, but most of them were not entertaining. For example, the Proletbuehne's 1932 agitprop, 15 Minute Red Salute, was a six-part revue composed of communist slogans written in dialogue with rhetorical questions and Marxist answers. "A good show might have been valuable as a political ritual, but the 15 Minute Red Salute was heavy-handed and dull."(2)

In contrast, feminist theatre's agitprops have been highly entertaining. The Welfare Wizard of Ours and Clown Wanted by the A & T, although dealing with serious matters of welfare and unemployment respectively, satirized social conditions through humor and variety acts. People enjoyed the playlets even if some disagreed with the politics. While not all communist agitprops were as bad as the 15 Minute Red Salute, they all were quite serious, aimed to teach and convert and clearly spoke the Communist Party's dogma.

By 1934, the Communist Party realized that agitprop was not defeating capitalism or even holding audiences, and it began producing plays with Marxist ideals woven into a realistic plot. However, the shift from political skits to drama with political content meant that good playwrights were needed.

The New Theatre League, formed in 1935 and formerly called the League of Workers' Theatres, loosely controlled a chain of theatres across the country and promised to supply them with good communist plays. This organization reached its zenith in its first season with the production of Clifford Odets' Waiting for Lefty, about a taxicab drivers' strike, which was performed by members of the Group Theatre.(3) Odets managed to combine the virtues of agitprop with a realistic plot that moved audiences on both the intellectual and emotional levels. However, except for some minor successes, including Irwin Shaw's Bury the Dead, the success of Waiting for Lefty was never repeated because the Party was unable to get good plays. Even the playwrights with communist sympathies preferred to be produced on Broadway, if possible, than to be given the sparse renderings of the poor New Theatre League.(4)

The shift from agitprop to realism, the lack of plays and the poverty are all paralleled in feminist theatres. While At the Foot of the Mountain has never performed agitprop, the other three groups did and moved from that form to combinations of agitprop and realism as in Battered Homes and Gardens and to realism as in Lady in the Corner and Cory.

Although there are several good feminist playwrights, feminist theatres have preferred to create their own plays in order to say exactly what they want to say in the way they want. While some of these collective pieces have been quite good, most suffer from having either too many authors or inexperienced authors. In any case the problem is the same as the communists faced--too few good plays.

The Communist Party, through the New Theatre League, had a national controlling organization and required its theatres to present communist plays which espoused the party line--the rise of the proletariat to crush capitalism. Feminist theatres have no national organization; indeed, most groups are unaware of other feminist theatres outside their own area. Nor do feminist theatre plays promote any single formula for the elimination of oppression. All seek to eliminate sexism and raise consciousness, but both form and content have been varied.

Communist theatre groups, like most present political theatres, were short-lived ventures, the average life span being five years. The A & T lasted five years; the Lavender Cellar existed two years, although it may resume activity; Circle of the Witch made it into a fifth year; and At the Foot of the Mountain is in its fifth year as a feminist theatre. The tensions of the work and inadequate finances undoubtedly foster such brief lives in spite of the dedication of members and the support of a political move-

ment.   However, in the case of the communist theatres,
World War II prosperity and the end of the Depression
brought about their demise.

> As symptoms of the economic disorder began to
> disappear toward the end of the thirties, the play-
> wright's prescriptions seemed more and more super-
> fluous.   The more spectacular return of American
> prosperity, brought on by the start of the wartime
> boom, destroyed the remaining theatrical aspirations
> of the American Communists.(5)

Another theatre of the 1930's the Federal Theatre,(6)
produced socio-political dramas, but its aims and means
were quite different from those of the communist theatres.
The Federal Theatre Project, begun in 1935, directed by
Hallie Flanagan, funded with a $6 million appropriation
from Congress and conceived as a Works Progress Administration (WPA) project to employ theatre workers, outlived
the communist theatres until it was killed by Congress in
1939, because it had become too politically controversial.
Actually non-political plays far outnumbered the Federal
Theatre's political offerings, yet it was reaction to the
political drama that brought about the project's demise.

> Unlike the communist theatres, the Federal Theatre
was a theatre first, not a propaganda tool, and exhibited
much variety in content and form even among its social
plays.

> Although Federal Theatre produced the Communist
> Revolt of the Beavers,   it   also   presented   such
> liberal   dramas   as   It Can't Happen Here.   The
> project offered plays that simply exposed a social
> problem, dramas that advocated reform, and one
> play that advocated revolution.   Federal Theatre
> offered the tragedy of Professor Mamlock, the fan-
> tasy of No More Peace, the farce of The Path of
> Flowers, and the romance of Big Blow....   And
> most important, it introduced to the new theatre
> movement the living newspaper, a form well suited
> to an effective and exciting theatrical analysis of
> society's problems.(7)

The Federal Theatre Project operated regional theatres across the United States, but control such as the
communists held was not exercised.   This project was well
financed and thus able to do things that communist theatres could not do.   Audiences liked the Federal Theatre's
productions and, in fact, this theatre absorbed the leftist
audience of the period.   The social message not only did
not dominate but was not as specific as the communist
content formula had been.   Finally, because the social

messages were presented subtly, a quality that annoyed communist reviewers, politics did not inhibit art.

The Federal Theatre, partly because of its success with audiences and partly because it could pay actors, technicians and playwrights, produced a higher quality of theatre than did other political theatres of the period. Significantly, it was able to attract first-rate playwrights which the communist theatres had never been able to do. Perhaps the most important thing about the Federal Theatre is that it gave people what they liked, not only what was good for them.

Although feminist theatres have neither the national organization nor the funding of the Federal Theatre, they are also not subject to demise by a congress or anyone else's dictate. As a specifically political theatre, feminist theatre has a more limited audience than the Federal Theatre had, but it definitely has a strong and supportive one. The dramatic variety presented by the Federal Theatre is paralleled in feminist theatre by its use of realism, expressionism, skits, revues, ritual, musicals, allegory, fantasy and satire to present a wide range of issues and concerns of women. Unlike the Federal Theatre, feminist theatre does not seek to be a theatre first. Rather, it equally emphasizes art and politics, realizing that good politics is no substitute for art. Plays of some groups have been in the popular forms, but few, except those intended as agitprop, have sacrificed theatre for didacticism. Feminist theatre attempts to give people what is good for them while concurrently entertaining them. What is good for them may simply be allowing an audience to see an artistic presentation of the woman's experience. Instead of a single party line as the communists advocated, there are several lines, and like the Federal Theatre's social plays, messages are consciousness raisers, not blueprints for action.(8)

While there are many parallels between feminist theatre and political theatre of the 1930's, ultimately there are more differences. Both the communist theatres and the Federal Theatre persisted in the established professional course, failing to conceive of or to realize a new vision for theatre as feminists have attempted. Collectivity in organization and playwriting, although advocated by the communists and present in the creation of the Federal Theatre's Living Newspapers, was virtually absent in these theatres. A significantly greater number of parallels exist between black theatre and feminist theatre, although, ironically, black theatres are mostly male dominated.

The Black Theatre Movement

After the 1930's, it took another 25 years for political theatre to reemerge. One important and distinct branch of such theatre was the black theatre or arts movement precipitated by a new black consciousness and civil rights issues.

Attitudes about blacks and theatre have radically changed in the last three decades. In 1947, Edith Isaacs, author of The Negro in the American Theatre, commented on a producton of Carmen Jones:

> The real test [of its success] was in the number of people who came away saying, "After the first half-hour I forgot that the actors were Negroes." ... It was another milestone passed toward the goal where the path of the Negro theatre would no longer be a separate road.(9)

Today, black theatre, like feminist theatre, is no longer seeking to blend with the mainstream. Like feminists, blacks believe they have been stereotyped, misrepresented or ignored in American drama and that if their experience is going to be truthfully presented, they are going to have to do it.

Blacks see the Harlem Renaissance of the 1920's as a failure because "it did not address itself to the mythology and life-styles of the black community."(10) With few exceptions, such as the Ebony Showcase,(11) black theatres reject the use of Negroes in white plays like Hello Dolly because these performances are viewed as simply hipper versions of minstrel shows. "They present Negroes acting out the hang-ups of middle-class white America."(12) Similarly many feminists have believed that traditional drama has been irrelevant or dangerous to women.

> Often what is "given" is opposed to the ideals we hold for ourselves and for the society we live in. The women invented for us are frequently a contradiction of what we know to be true of our inner selves, and thus in a peculiar way we become the perpetrators of the status quo and the roles created for us rather than by us.(13)

Black theatre, which is by, for and about blacks, is paralleled by feminist theatre which is primarily by, for and about women. Substitutions, indicated by words in brackets, in the following article on the black arts movement will reveal how similar these two theatres are.

> The Black Arts Movement [feminist theatre] is radically opposed to any concept of the artist that alienates him [her or him] from his [her or his] community. Black Art [feminist art] is the aes-

thetic and spiritual sister of the Black Power [wom-
en's liberation] concept. As such, it envisions an
art that speaks directly to the needs and aspira-
tions of Black America [women]. In order to perform this task, the Black Arts Movement [feminist
theatre] proposes a radical reordering of the Western Cultural aesthetic.... Currently, these [black]
[feminist] writers are re-evaluating western aesthetics, the traditional role of the writer, and the
social function of art. Implicit in this re-evaluation
is the need to develop a Black [feminist] aesthetic.(14)

Both the black and the feminist movements have
spawned and nurtured many good playwrights; however,
both groups of writers in the past have had problems in
determining for whom to write. Women writers realized
that getting their works produced would be more difficult
if the plays were too woman oriented.(15)

One of the major dilemmas of many earlier Negro
playwrights and theatres was their preoccupation
with the white audience, which required them to
explain their terminology, protest their condition,
prove their humility and generally pander to the
tastes of the white majority.(16)

Today, most feminist and black writers and theatres
have decided on a primary audience, and many theatres of
both kinds have purposefully located themselves near their
audiences. Black theatre groups work in black neighborhoods or areas, and feminist groups often operate out
of women's centers.

Another problem shared by black and feminist theatres is that of performing or creating works dealing with
oppression and the reactions of its victims. While often
only an initial, angry, overt stage through which writers
and groups pass, drama that verbally flagellates the enemy
often fails to portray the woman's or the black's experience. Micki Massimino's comments, quoted in Chapter IV,
about the creation of Sexpot Follies, and her group's
subsequent move toward focusing on women in its next
play, Lady in the Corner, illustrates the point. Adam
Miller takes issue with many black dramas, including James
Baldwin's Blues for Mister Charlie, Douglas Turner Ward's
Day of Absence and Lorraine Hansberry's A Raisin in the
Sun. Of the latter play, Miller comments:

In short, Miss Hansberry is saying to a white
audience: here are the Youngers, a good American
family operating in the tradition of thrift and hard
work, the trademark of successful mobility in the
society. They only want a chance to prove to you

what good neighbors they can be. Why don't you
let them?(17)

While black theatre artists wrestle with problems
within and without the theatre, they are attempting to
create new forms and contents, discover a black acting
technique,(18) utilize psychological tools for increasing
awareness and expression,(19) organize work on a collective
basis,(20) and write collectively and create black
rituals.(21)   These goals and methods, as well as variety
in drama, are also found in feminist theatres.

Another comparison of black and feminist theatre
relates to money. Both have little. Black theatres have
received more grants because they have been requesting
them longer and because special poverty programs have
funded them.   Both theatres have managed to survive on
limited budgets with little financial reward, but how long
such energy can last is a question which must be faced
not only by the theatres, but by the audiences and movements they serve.

Finally, black and feminist theatres differ in their
opinions of who or what is responsible for their oppression.
Black drama, when it lays blame, puts it squarely upon
whites. Feminist drama, at least that coming from groups
that have transcended the man-hating stage, tends to
blame the social system which men control but in which
women participate. Feminists see both sexual and racial
oppression as stemming from a common source, while blacks
have been reluctant to align their cause with any other.
Indeed, black women have often had to choose between the
black movement and the feminist movement; it is this
dilemma that prompted the founding of the National Black
Feminist Organization in 1973.(22)

Both feminist and black theatres are for the most part
remaining separate for the time being in order to explore
and understand their own histories, cultures and experiences.   Hopefully, in the future, minority and women's
theatres will exist to present the experiences special to
these groups, not in protest to an oppressive social order.

Since its beginning in the early 1960's as a distinct
type of theatre, black theatre has changed and developed
and is now a significant and internationally recognized
minority theatre. Feminist theatre, younger by a decade,
is only beginning to exert influence and achieve recognition. However, even in this early stage some observations can be made, trends noted and prophecies made. In
fact, the following observations on feminist theatre may be
compared to studies of black theatre done ten years ago
which were only able to suggest the important place in
theatre that blacks would make for themselves. Startling

revelations about feminist theatre are not discernible at this time, but observations made now are important in relationship to subsequent research and studies which are certain to appear.

Chapter VII

OBSERVATIONS ON FEMINIST THEATRE

Having decribed the ideologies and activities of four Minneapolis feminist theatre groups and having compared and contrasted them with one another and with other political theatres, it is possible to make some concluding observations on the phenomenon. First, there is an important relationship between the women's movement and feminist theatre. Second, the drama written and produced by theatre companies has exhibited a number of comparable traits. Next, in spite of its youth, feminist theatre is not without unique qualities, original methods and a number of successes to its credit. Feminist theatre criticism, itself a burgeoning field, is an important aspect of feminist theatre developed in response to the appearance of this new women's theatre. Last, observations on problems feminist theatres face and on future prospects for such companies have been made in the belief that feminist theatre has a future, possibly a great one.

Feminist Theatre and the Women's Movement

Undoubtedly, feminist theatre groups are a reflection of the political movement that gave them impetus. While groups are rarely affiliated with any official movement organization, they have absorbed the consciousness of the movement and applied it to their theatres.

Consciousness-raising sessions, insituted by the movement as an initial, personal technique for women to learn about the nature of their oppression, have been employed by groups to facilitate ingroup communication and to aid in the development of theatre pieces which in turn act as consciousness raisers for an audience.

Consciousness raising cultivates anger, an understandable stage of incipient feminist awareness, in both women and theatre groups. Both usually transcend this stage, theatre groups moving to exploration of the woman's

93

experience through drama. The women's movement is
concerned with exposing female myths, shattering female
stereotypes and providing role models for women. Likewise feminist theatre seeks to discover what a woman is
and could be, values the woman's experience, creates
accurate characterizations and establishes a woman's tradition through a rediscovery and reappraisal of women's
history.

The movement and its theatres support women and
foster sisterhood. Theatre groups are close-knit organizations and the bottom line of many plays establishes that
by working together women will more quickly achieve their
goals. The women's movement has taught to all its parts
the concept of collectivity in response to the existent hierarchical, competitive power structure, and its theatres
have almost universally adopted it.

The movement and theatres alike wish to deepen the
commitment of feminists and to win non-feminists to their
point of view. Conversion tactics, which begin with
consciousness raising, are subtle; feminist drama is often
visionary but it is rarely prescriptive.

Feminist theatre and feminism are emerging and there
is much variety in its ways and means. The movement's
extremes, conservative and radical, are paralleled by two
distinct types of feminist theatre. Conservative feminists
seek reform within the present social structure and conservative theatres primarily provide work opportunities for
women in theatre. For example, the Interart Theatre in
New York showcases women's work, providing necessary
experience, encouragement, exposure and recognition as
well as employment. These "conservative" theatres operate
much like traditional theatres and frequently act as aven-
ues for women into mainstream theatre work.

The radical segment of the women's movement seeks a
fundamental change in the social system. Most feminist
theatres, including those in Minneapolis, are of this type.
They are organized on the principles of radical feminism,
are as dedicated to politics as to art, support movement
activities and do not strive for individual or group success
according to most established criteria.(1)

The close comparison of feminist theatre with the
women's movement reveals this theatre's desire to merge its
ethics with its aesthetics.

Feminist Drama

Feminist theatre is immensely varied. Almost every
style there is can be used to express something about
women. Currently, most although not all feminist drama

deals with the oppression of a woman or group of women.
Usually the ending of a play shows the protagonists reaching some new awareness. Plays such as Cory, Lady
in the Corner and River Journal are examples; these, like
most others, do not show how the newly aware characters
will function in a still sexist world. Perhaps the solutions
are too complex. Deborah Fortson of the Commonplace
Pageant says:

> When people see a struggle without an answer, they
> get upset because they want a positive answer. I
> think a positive answer exists in a clearly posed
> question. A solution which is too simple for a
> complex situation is not believable and gives the
> audience a false sense of knowing what to do.(2)

Whatever the content, it is personal or as Joanna
Russ calls it, "fictional myths, growing out of their
lives,"(3) and sometimes it is autobiographical. In the
past, the terms personal and autobiographical, when de-
scribing women's art, were derogatory terms because they
implied a lack of authentic creativity. Gloria Orenstein
comments:

> Today we are beginning to understand that male art
> is also partly autobiographical, but that, whereas
> the subject matter of men's lives was traditionally
> sanctioned, there was a taboo and a prejudice
> against the subject matter of women's lives....
> Male critics are willing to accept photo-realist
> paintings of motorcycles and automobiles, but are
> simply unwilling to accept paintings of perfume
> bottles, jewels, or anything that suggests the
> content of a woman's life-style.(4)

Woman now are refusing to accept this kind of value judg-
ment and are writing about universal experiences from
their own and other women's experiences.

While every female experience is subject to artistic
representation, several seem to be more popular among
feminist theatre groups. Mother-daughter relationships
have been examined by each Minneapolis group, especially
in Circle of the Witch's Lady in the Corner and At the
Foot of the Mountain's Pimp, River Journal and The Story
of a Mother. Other plays on this theme include the Rhode
Island Feminist Theatre's Persephone's Return, Womanrite's
Daughters, Honor Moore's Mourning Pictures, Ursule
Molinaro's Breakfast Past Noon and Megan Terry's Calm
Down Mother.

Women's history plays, ranging from panoramas of
whole periods to biographies of real or imagined women,
have been widely successfully produced by feminist theatres. Circle of the Witch's Time Is Passing, the Alive and

Trucking Theatre's The People Are a River, the Co-
Respondents' Here She Comes, the Rhode Island Feminist
Theatre's Anne Hutchinson, the Open Stage's Eleanor!,
Marie! and Sisters of Liberty, Roma Greth's President's
Daughter/President's Wife, Marisa Geoffre's Bread and
Roses, Megan Terry's Approaching Simone, Ruth Wolff's
The Abdication, Gloria Goldsmith's Womanspeak and Karen
Malpede's Rebeccah are some of the many plays that seek
to reclaim women's lost history and suggest role models for
contemporary women. (See List of Plays Cited, at the end
of the book, for information on these and other works
mentioned.)

       Commonplace activities and images, prevalent in visual
art by women, are frequently represented in feminist
drama, sometimes in an effort to point out the value of
acts ordinarily perceived as trivial, sometimes to point out
the terrible waste involved in them. Two distinct examples
exist in the Commonplace Pageant's Baggage which por-
trays the drama of everyday struggles and in Judy Chicago's group's Ironing and Waiting in which actresses
simply iron and wait.

       Among other topics are rape, women in prison, women
and madness, aging women, male/female relationships,
social problems of daycare, unemployment, problems of
welfare and urban renewal, and lesbianism.

       Women's fantasies have been explored in Pig in a
Blanket and River Journal, and the Commonplace Pageant's
Mermaids, Circle of the Witch's The Changebringers and
Joanna Russ's Window Dressing are all subtitled fantasy
plays. However, few plays have deeply explored women's
imaginations or subliminal experiences. Perhaps as women
continue to write from their personal experiences, women's
private sides and special experiences will be more thor-
oughly explored. Roberta Sklar comments:

       There are certain experiences that we've hardly
       been allowed to have, and there are some experi-
       ences that we've had which have been pushed into
       a place that is different from the place we really
       experienced it. For example, childbirth.... One
       of the things I think would be really interesting to
       get into in terms of new content for women's the-
       atre is some more of the unknown experiences that
       we've had. And they're not about rejecting men or
       being hostile about having been oppressed.
       They're about re-establishing the meaningfulness of
       certain events of our lives.(5)

In order to develop this kind of personal material,
writers or theatres must have a supporting, trusting
environment in which to risk exposing their emotions and

experiences. Feminist theatres and feminist audiences are now providing this trust and support. Playwright Karen Malpede says:

> I have always felt that none of my plays could have been written were it not for the close working relationships I have had with the actors and directors of the previous play.... The playwright who works with such actors maintains a joyous responsibility to delve deep into the areas of self where the changes happen, so that, in hours of rehearsal her words and structures can be given living form and then, through the actors' abandonment to the need of the moment, can breathe the transcendent life of change into an audience.(6)

It is reasonable to expect that the woman playwright will be more willing to take greater risks in expressing herself as she becomes "free to oppose the male-oriented view of reality with imagery and thematic material arising from the authenticity of her sensual experience."(7)

Feminist critics maintain that drama and theatre have falsely portrayed or ignored women in the past. How then does feminist drama portray women and men? What images of both sexes are apparent?

Although each play's characters are different and must be considered within the drama in which they appear, a large number of plays show women in the midst of identity crises. The heroine is dissatisfied, angry, confused and on the brink of some new awareness about herself and her role as a woman. The dramatic conflict arises out of how she will react to and solve her dilemma. Interestingly, a number of plays have not one but several female protagonists, a trend paralleled in novels by women. Whatever her function in the play, the woman acts according to her own desires, dreams and motivations and not out of stereotyped perceptions of what a woman should do or be.

Male characters are usually treated sympathetically in feminist drama as agents and victims in an oppressive social order. However, since attention is focused on the female characters, there are few significant male roles. The general lack of numbers of male characters is also in part due to the fact that many plays are written and/or performed by all female companies.

One dominant characteristic of feminist drama is the use of short forms or one-act plays. As reasons for this playwrights indicate inexperience, lack of skill to sustain a longer piece and the fact that some plays were written for presentation at gatherings where a longer play would be unsuitable. Megan Terry, who has written many plays of an hour or less in length, says that she wants "to say it,

get it over with and go on to the next thing."(8) Myrna
Lamb says that shorter plays are easier to get produced
and that her intense, compact, direct style is suited to
her material which often deals with situations already
familiar to audiences.(9) Michelene Wandor agrees with
Lamb that it is easier to find venues for short plays, and
she believes that "the expressionistic element, when present, is often more effective in the one act form."(10)

   Plotless, circular, layered, poetic, choral, lyric,
primal, ritual-like, multi-climactic, surreal, mosaic, collage-
like and non-realistic are terms often used to describe the
bulk of feminist drama. Feminist writers seem to have
rejected traditional "male" forms, which are built on a
hierarchical dramatic structure. According to Megan
Terry, plays by men out of the Greek tradition are built
on a male pyramid, and "all the characters around this one
male show only one aspect of themselves, usually in support or opposition to this creature."(11) Joanna Russ
notes that the groups of protagonists in many women's
novels and plays allow the presentation of more complicated
interrelationships with several people on a level.(12)

   In A Room of One's Own Virginia Woolf points out
that by the time women began writing there were definite
myths and structures already established.(13) However,
these forms did not often suit what women were writing
about. Joanna Russ believes that the circular, plotless
forms which she calls lyricism have been adopted because
they do fit the content women are writing about. She
states:

> If the narrative mode (what Aristotle called "epic")
> concerns itself with events connected by the chron-
> ological order in which they occur, and the dra-
> matic mode with voluntary human actions which are
> connected both by chronology and causation, then
> the principle of construction I wish to call lyric
> consists of the organization of discrete elements
> (images, events, scenes, passages, words, what-
> have-you) around an unspoken thematic or emotional
> center. The lyric mode exists without chronology
> or causation; its principle of connection is
> associative.
> The problem of "outsider" artists is the whole
> problem of what to do with unlabeled, disallowed,
> disavowed, not-even-consciously-perceived experi-
> ence, experience which cannot be spoken about
> because it has no embodiment in existing art.
> Hence the lyric structure, which can deal with
> the unspeakable and unembodyable as its thematic
> center, or the realistic piling up of detail which

> may (if you are lucky) eventually add up to the
> unspeakable, undramatizable, unembodyable, action-
> one-cannot-name.(14)

This cyclic, rhythmic, illogical lyric form relates well to
the intuitive, emotional source of much of women's drama
and reflects the contemporary woman's emergent status and
search for a way to name the unnameable.

New plays by women which use this form listed by
Honor Moore in a recent article on feminist theatre include
Elizabeth Swado's Nightclub Cantata, Eve Merriam's Viva
Reviva and The Club, Sarah Kernochan's Pranks for
Warped Children and Myrna Lamb's Mother Ann.

> Other works, like Susan Griffin's Voices and
> [Ntozake] Shange's Colored Girls ... are written in
> poetry for female voices and have no conventional
> plot. Still others are plays with several or at least
> a duet of female main characters: Megan Terry's
> Babes in the Bighouse, Liz Stern's ... Unfinished
> Women, Uncommon Women, Leigh Curran's Lunch
> Girls, and Anne Burr's play in progress, Solid
> State....
> For me, these forms represent an antihierarchical
> move away from the male-invented "leading lady"
> isolated in her predicament, and a return to the
> all-female chorus which some scholars claim may
> have preceded the male chorus of Greek
> tragedy.(15)

It is too soon to identify an original form in feminist
drama precisely because women are still experimenting with
and searching for forms that appeal to them. "for masterpieces are not single and solitary births; they are the
outcome of many years of thinking in common, of thinking
by the body of the people, so that the experiences of the
mass is behind the single voice."(16) The woman artist's
and writer's problem is very related to the fact that she
has no tradition to rely on, or one so short and partial
that it is inadequate.(17)

Unique Aspects of Feminist Theatre

The principal original aspect of feminist theatre is
that it exists. There has never before been a feminist
theatre; the phenomenon is unprecedented.

Second, feminist theatres are presenting truthful
images of women and the woman's experience through a
growing body of drama that specifically focuses on women.
The originality of these occurrences is significant because
throughout history women have been falsely portrayed,

stereotyped, shown only in relation to males or ignored altogether, facts well documented since the advent of feminist criticism.(18)

The feminist renaissance and theatres growing out of it have provided both a market for theatre about women and an environment where such work can be developed. Theatre is especially suitable art for women because through acting (role playing) they can break social barriers and have experiences routinely denied them in real life.(19) Thus the theatre can be cathartic for actors and for audiences who identify with the drama. Once experienced in the safe, illusory theatre, ideas and acts can more easily be transferred to life.

One trend occurring in feminist theatre is the use of negative female images in new positive ways. The dark private sphere, the hysteria, "our emotionalism, our irrationalism, that whole horrific archetypal horror picture of the woman"(20) is being exposed and used. Groups such as At the Foot of the Mountain are exploring these so-called female traits in workshops and putting their discoveries into their work as in The Moon Tree, about women's insanity, and River Journal, which explores one woman's psyche.

The rationale behind such explorations contends, at least in part, that negative images and behaviors exist for reasons. Feminists want to show why such behavior is present in women. Stereotyped female characters are not hysterical or bitchy for any reason. "There is no explanation in terms of human motivation or the woman's own inner life; she simply behaves the way she does because she is a bitch."(21)

Further, feminists believe that these "feminine aspects" may not be negative at all when presented from the woman's perspective. Just as blacks have dealt with the nigger image, women have claimed the full range of their emotions in order to free themselves from externally imposed stereotypes.

Another somewhat similar unique function of feminist theatre is that it is often a communal art experience, a function which most theatres have ceased to fulfill in any real sense. It is communal because it is live, is dedicated to an ideology that fosters sisterhood and is alert to the value of audience-performer interaction.

Because of the varying makeup of audiences, not all feminist performances are communal events. However, performances, especially celebratory and ritualistic ones, at which the audience is all or predominantly female and/or feminist, vastly increase the potential for such a group event. While few men would enjoy the communal benefits of feminist theatre, most can appreciate its consciousness raising functions.

Collectivity, as a mode of operation or method of playwriting, is not new, but it has led to the new awareness that different techniques in acting--a women's acting method--are possible. Groups such as Circle of the Witch and At the Foot of the Mountain suggest that the best approach to acting for women may be different from that for men because of differences in socialization. They are in the process of discovering and identifying such a method based on women's emotional responses to their personal experiences such as memories, dreams and wishes. Logical analysis gives way to intuitive, emotional reaction.

Collective organization is responsible for the large number of collaborative plays in feminist drama. Not only have women in the past rarely written with even a co-author, but no other experimental/political theatre has so extensively relied on collective playwriting.

It may be premature to name ritual as an original or unique aspect of feminist theatre, yet one cannot avoid noticing the many elements of ritual in feminist drama and the many women's celebrations and rites being performed by theatre groups. While most performances of this nature, including At the Foot of the Mountain's River Journal and the Rhode Island Feminist Theatre's Persephone's Return, only use elements of ritual or incorporate rites into the play, others such as Rites of Women's Womanritual and Rites of Passage and At the Foot of the Mountain's Spring Equinox Celebration are more ritual than drama. Carol Grosberg comments:

> It's [women's theatre] really a sacred art and movement--it touches on the deepest and most universal experiences, and there's a way in which we're finding our way back to the origins of art which lie in a sort of religious expression.
>
> [Political theatre of the women's movement] does have to do with exploring our sickness and understanding it and exorcising it and finding new forms and in a kind of intuitive way discovering them. The origins of myths is in ritual.... We're sort of coming back to that. It's not a going backwards, but it's a finding of those deepest places and finding them for ourselves in the context of Western society.(22)

One member of At the Foot of the Mountain explains ritual in the company's collaborative piece, The Story of a Mother:

> We are our mothers' daughters. We want to reclaim this relationship, to honor and explore its

> importance in our lives. We are working to do this
> through a dramatized ritual event, a journey of
> sorts on which you as an audience member will be
> invited to come to witness your own relationship to
> your own mothers and daughters, to rejoice in them
> or scream about them, to forgive perhaps, or to
> simply see them for what they are. As we work on
> this drama every day, we discover more about it
> and witness it emerge as a healing ritual event. In
> January and February we will take parts of it to
> groups in the community who perhaps have no
> experience in theatre, but who will bring their own
> life-experiences to the piece and respond accord-
> ingly. Thus we hope to create The Story of a
> Mother in concert with the community, tapping the
> shared feelings of all mothers, daughters, and
> families around this central bond.(23)

Women's myths or "story patterns" may evolve from these
ritual performances.

> Writers do not make up their plots out of thin air;
> they are pretty much restricted to the attitudes,
> the beliefs, the expectations, and above all the
> plots, that are "in the air"--"plot" being what
> Aristotle called mythos; and in fact it is probably
> most accurate to call these plot-patterns myths.(24)

To the degree our culture is male dominated, our
myths are male centered. For many myths, at least Western ones, simple gender reversal will make this clear. It
is this lack of a strong female mythic heritage that is
perhaps most responsible for the tendency of women
writers to rely on the lyric form. From whatever source,
new myths must come.

> The lack of workable myths ... of acceptable dra-
> matizations of what our experience means, harms
> much more than the art itself. We do not only
> choose or reject works of art on the basis of these
> myths; we interpret our own experience in terms of
> them. Worse still, we actually perceive what hap-
> pens to us in the mythic terms our culture
> provides.(25)

Changes in consciousness, perception and culture may
naturally produce new myths. Ritual can also create
myths, and theatre groups such as At the Foot of the
Mountain, Circle of the Witch, Rites of Women, Womanrite,
New Cycle Theatre, Motion, Rhode Island Feminist Theatre
and Spiderwoman are attempting to develop the communal,
emotional, intuitive, and spiritual aspects of their theatres
to explain part of the world view of women, to complete
the incomplete cycle, to satisfy unsatisfied desires and to

provide outlets for emotions and perceptions that have not found vents in practical action.(26)

Successes of Feminist Theatre

Most feminist theatre groups reject traditional success measurements, and measuring success by the groups' standards, such as ability to affect an audience with feminist material, would necessitate extensive, complicated audience surveys. How, then, can the groups' progress be assessed? Feminist theatres have been working for nearly ten years and are growing. The December 1977 issue of Ms. listed 14 additional feminist theatres, none of which was included in its 1975 survey.(27) While feminist theatre audiences are not large, they compare favorably with audiences of other fringe theatres and have grown each year. Feminist theatres have made their work accessible to sectors of the public that rarely experience plays, through tours and performances not only in theatres but wherever an audience could be gathered.

Feminist theatre groups have continued to receive public and private grants, reflecting their stability and the acceptance of their work as a valid art form. However, groups have resisted compromising their ideals for any reason, fame and money notwithstanding. The dedication and commitment of group members must be counted among the successes of feminist theatre.

Finally, feminist theatre has had some effect on mainstream theatre. According to Meri Golden, formerly of the Alive and Trucking Theatre Company and now working in meainstream theatre, women from feminist groups who go on to work in establishment theatres bring with them a kind of consciousness about theatre that affects the establishment group.(28) Martha Boesing believes that the fact that there have been more than one feminist theatres in Minneapolis has influenced Minneapolis mainstream theatres both in hiring practicies and play selection.(29) Barbara Field, literary manager for the Guthrie Theatre,(30) and Emily Mann, a Guthrie director,(31) agree that while theatre in Minneapolis is still male dominated, feminist theatres are being noticed and are having some influence on the city's theatrical offerings. In New York Ntozake Shange's Spell #7, Mary O'Malley's Once a Catholic, Marsha Norman's Getting Out, Rose Leiman Goldemberg's Letters Home, Pat Carroll's Gertrude Stein Gertrude Stein Gertrude Stein, Susan Dworkin's Deli's Fable and Nancy Ford's I'm Getting My Act Together and Taking It on the Road were among the dramatic offerings by women in the fall of 1979.

Feminists have successfully used theatre as a means to combine public and private experiences to promote radical change when other means have been closed.

> In conflicts where competing groups have vastly unequal power, the weak group often finds trad- itional forms of argument and public discourse inadequate. Low power groups, therefore, often resort to techniques of violent confrontation and/or symbolic protest.(32)

Women have rejected violence, but have adopted symbolic protest, especially through theatre. "Theatre, itself a kind of symbol, has the ability to present events which appear real while retaining control and prescribing out- comes."(33)

Feminist theatre is a grassroots theatre that has managed to survive without national organization. Based on experimentation or trial and error, groups have devel- oped means for the discovery and correction of errors. Through their discussions and analyses, groups have learned how to better combine political ideology with art. One of the successes of feminist theatre has been the definite trend away from simplistic agitprop to artistic, sophisticated social drama. While most groups find agit- prop useful at times, they have recognized the greater potential of art. Martha Boesing comments:

> Agitprop just looks at the problem. There is some way it makes both the oppressor and the oppressed "other." Agitprop is always about other people, not me. I can never see in agitprop that it is terrible what I am doing to myself, and therefore to others, and what others are doing to me.(34)

As shown in this book, the Minneapolis feminist theatres made definite moves away from agitprop toward concen- trating on perfecting women's theatre art.

Feminist Theatre Criticism

The question of whether or not a feminist aesthetic exists looms large in feminist criticism. While theatre groups have not been too concerned with the issue, play- wrights, reviewers, critics and historians have. Many feminist playwrights, including Susan Yankowitz, Megan Terry and Myrna Lamb, are against the formulation of an aesthetic because of implicit restrictions that would be disastrous to an emerging art form. However, Martha Boesing believes that if women are going to develop a counterculture that is literally not any part of our culture (because the whole culture is male) "then you have got to have people who say, 'That is feminist and that's not.'"(35)

> The answer to the questions of whether, indeed
> there is something definable as a "female aesthetic"
> is ultimately less important than the fact that the
> issue has been raised, for it means that contempor-
> ary women are taking art history into their own
> hands and molding it to suit their own image. If
> there is to be a bio-aesthetic, a uniquely female
> style of artistic expression, many of these women
> have taken the first steps necessary for its
> creation.(36)

Feminist theatre companies, if unconcerned about aesthetics, are concerned about reviews of their work and
that criticism avoid making universal statements based on
male experience. Nancy Sugarman of Circle of the Witch
believes that it is important for critics, first, to value the
woman's experience and, second, to understand and value
what is being attempted.(37) Martha Boesing of At the
Foot of the Mountain sees the potential for criticism of
feminist plays as being to teach the public how to see
them.(38) Since values are crucial in criticism, the question arises as to whether or not a non-feminist, especially
a non-feminist male, can adequately evaluate feminist
theatre.

Drama critic Marilyn Stasio says that she does not
think that plays by or about women demand special treat-
ment but reveals, through an examination of criticism of
three plays, how women's drama has been insensitively
reviewed by media critics, most of whom are male. For
example, reviews of Anne Burr's Mert & Phil elicited a
barrage of abusive and hostile remarks from New York
male critics. Stasio admits the play had problems, but the
violent overreaction of the reviewers, she says, was due
to the threat to males and their values posed by the female
protagonist, Mert.

> Burr was violently denounced by critics who still
> cherish the very values she is questioning. Neither
> evil nor vindictive men, the critics illustrated an
> imbalanced and limited perception. They were
> caught off-guard by an attack on the values they
> hold dear and are afraid or unwilling to question
> themselves. And the playwright, whatever the
> artistic flaws of this play, was denied the encour-
> agement, respect, and admiration she has at the
> very least deserved.

Critic Margaret Lamb also notes distortion and lack of
understanding in criticism of women's plays and advises
the following:

(a)   Sustained visionary work by a critic who
believes that feminist theatre has a possibly great
future as a revolutionary but undogmatic approach
to the art.

(b)   Criticism which could examine the "woman
question" in the theatre the way Marxist critic
George Lukács examined class in the novel, without
jargon and within the broadest possible historical
and cultural context.

(c)   Citicism of critics, particularly of what they
leave out.

(d)   Technical criticism of the commercial theatre
that reveals unconscious attitudes and values.

(e)   Coverage of specifically feminist theatre in
other countries, particularly those in which the
position of women is lowest.(40)

If women have had to create their own theatres in
order to express their experience accurately, unfortunately
it follows that they will have to develop their own critics
to evaluate that work. Feminist critics are needed not to
promote an ingroup "hooray for our side" kind of thinking
but to comment objectively on a new kind of theatre that
they understand because of their dual understanding of
feminism and of theatre.

Problems for Feminist Theatres

Feminist theatre groups face several major problems,
most of which are common to small theatres in general:
money, isolation, audience, membership and writers.

The very survival of groups is related to the lack of
funds, as the brief lifespan of many groups attests. If
feminist theatre is to become a stable art and compete with
mainstream theatre, it must be able to support itself and
its members. The corollaries to the dearth of money are
the lack of time to explore and develop adequately a
uniquely female theatre and the lack of technical support.
Since most companies wish also to appeal to low-income
people, income from box office cannot be expected to
alleviate the situation. Subsidies seem to be the only
answer at this time. However, while many groups are
being partially funded, such funds are not enough or even
comparable to grants being awarded to small establishment
theatres.

A second problem is related to the isolation of feminist theatre groups. Of all groups surveyed, few knew
of more than three feminist theatres operating outside their
own geographical area. Groups need to see one another's

work and have the opportunity to discuss methods, to encourage and support each other and to establish a clearinghouse for the ideas and drama of feminist theatre. Groups might also unite to get large grants from national endowments. That individual groups, already overworked, do not want to invest the necessary time to set up a national network is understandable. However, there may already be mechanisms established, such as the American Theatre Association's Women's Program or one of the women's art or research centers, which could fulfill this function. Feminist theatres do not need a bureaucracy; they do need national communication, support and recognition.

All theatres aim for a primary audience mainly through the plays they produce and the prices they charge. Audience selection is difficult for feminist theatres because of their political commitment. Should they appeal primarily to women? to feminists? to non feminists? to low-income people? to people? Inasmuch as the activities of a theatre relate directly to its audience, some decision must be made. The kind and level of persuasion present is the key. Certainly a feminist performance for high school students will differ from one intended for a mixed theatre audience or for a lesbian group or for a women's club. It is not necessary that every group appeal to the same audience or that every play of a single group appeal to the same audience, but failure to identify the primary audience may result in the failure to appeal to anybody.

For the most part the Minneapolis groups each decided on an audience: the Alive and Trucking sought a broad audience, especially of working-class people; the Lavender Cellar successfully appealed to the lesbian community; At the Foot of the Mountain and Circle of the Witch have been less specific in their audience choices, although the former appears to appeal largely to feminist women. Circle of the Witch states, perhaps naively, that it wishes to perform "for people."

It is important to note that the broad, general feminist theatre audience makeup is very related to the fact that these groups are available for hire. While many other theatre groups conduct national and regional tours, few maintain a repertory from which special interest groups or institutions can select a play for one performance. Even the ubiquitous San Francisco Mime Troupe has played to a less diverse audience than have most feminist theatres which have performed for hospitals, prisons, parks, women's organizations of all kinds, colleges, public and private schools, union meetings, neighborhood organizations, cooperatives, school faculties, lawyer's guilds, conventions, women's centers, churches, senior citizens, unwed mother's homes, orphanages and even television.

Membership can be a problem for feminist theatres because they must contend with problems of inequality of ability in their members and the constant need for replacement of members who leave. While the Minneapolis groups had no problem keeping a stable membership averaging seven members, many groups consist of only three people because time and work demands are great and pay is low or nonexistent.

An adjunct problem concerns admitting men. If men are admitted to membership, groups may lose their feminist focus since power is equally shared and male members may not be content to do women's plays everlastingly. The A & T, which lost its feminist orientation after two years, is a case in point. However, without male actors there are some plays which cannot be performed and some experiences which cannot be shown. Several groups have solved the problem by working with male actors for specific productions but not admitting them to the group as members. A much less successful solution was found by the Lavender Cellar which cast women in the male roles in Cory.

The major problem for feminist theatres is the lack of first-rate plays. Mostly, feminist theatre companies are either collectively writing their own plays or are working with a member-playwright. Collective playwriting is not inherently bad, but as Karen Malpede points out, "the quality of the language usually suffers and, therefore, so does the depth and breadth of the acting."(41) Plays may suffer from too many authors, but more often from the fact that the creators are not writers. Good plays are a necessity for any theatre and if feminist theatres wish to ignore the drama of outside feminist playwrights, they must develop playwriting skills.

Another problem with collective writing is that groups are prone to begin with a message or statement of purpose as the A & T always did. This approach may work for agitprop skits and historical documentaries, but elsewhere it means that the message is superimposed rather than organic. Groups that insist on extending the philosophy of collective organization to playwriting might find a suitable compromise in having the acting ensemble work with a playwright, if one is available, to create a piece that expresses the members' feelings but is finally shaped by one vision.

Future Prospects for Feminist Theatre

Feminist theatre groups are of three basic types, although there is some overlap among them. One group wishes to develop women's talents for subsequent use in mainstream theatres, another promotes woman-oriented feminist theatres within the male-dominated structure, and a third is interested in matriarchal theatres.

For this third type to exist would require a social revolution, for it implies either a large separatist female culture or a move by the whole society away from patriarchal values, neither of which has occurred yet. Such a theatre will always oppose the status quo until it becomes the status quo.

The other two types operate within the current social system supported by the various movements working for sex equality. Which kind of women's theatre ultimately dominates will be determined by the rate and type of social change. Joanna Russ comments:

> One thing I think we must know--that our traditional gender roles will not be part of the future, as long as the future is not a second Stone Age. Our traditions, our books, our morals, our manners, our films, our speech, our economic organization, everything we have inherited, tells us that to be a Man one must bend Nature to one's will--or other men. This means ecological catastrophe in the first instance and war in the second. To be a Woman, one must be first and foremost a mother and after that a server of Men; this means overpopulation and the perpetuation of the first two disasters. The roles are deadly. The myths that serve them are fatal.(42)

Feminist art and literature are attempting to mirror and give resonance to woman's experience, to present the other point of view. Out of such efforts positive social change may come about providing new roles and new myths.

That feminist theatre exists is the most important observation one can make at this point because it means that women are saying "no." Camus asks:

> What is a rebel? A man [woman] who says no.... [T]he movement of rebellion is founded simultaneously on the categorical rejection of an intrusion that is considered intolerable and on the confused conviction of an absolute right which, in the rebel's mind, is more precisely the impression that he [she] "has the right to...."(43)

Women in feminist theatre are rebels who repudiate previous perceptions and formulations about women and in the very act of saying no, make a positive statement. Implicit in every no is a yes; yes there are alternatives.

Women's theatre and art are still young. To expect masterpieces or even to be able to recognize them if they

do appear is not yet reasonable. However, the first step
has been taken. Camus continued:

> Awareness, no matter how confused it may be,
> develops from every act of rebellion: the sudden,
> dazzling perception that there is something in man
> [woman] with which he [she] can identify himself
> [herself], even if only for a moment.(44)

This new awareness, however confused, has prompted
numerous women in theatre for the first time to discover
and express their own values about women, art and life.

CHAPTER NOTES

Chapter I

1. Arthur Sainer, The Radical Theatre Notebook (New York: Avon Books, 1975), pp. xii-xiv.

2. Henry Lesnick, ed., Guerilla Street Theatre (New York: Avon Books, 1973), p. 11.

3. Françoise Kourilsky and Leonora Champagne, "Political Theatre in France Since 1968," Drama Review, 19 (June 1975), 44.

4. Robert Pasolli, A Book on the Open Theatre (Indianapolis: Bobbs-Merrill, 1970).

5. Jessica B. Harris, "The National Black Theatre," Drama Review 16 (December 1972), 39-45.

6. Pierre Biner, The Living Theatre (New York: Horizon Press, 1972).

7. Marlow Hotchkiss, Firehouse Theatre (Minneapolis: By the Author, 1969).

8. Richard Schechner, Environmental Theatre (New York: Hawthorne Books, 1973).

9. Karen Malpede Taylor, People's Theatre in Amerika (New York: Drama Book Specialists, 1972), p. 210.

10. Sainer, The Radical Theatre Notebook, pp. 15-16.

11. Michael Kirby, "On Political Theatre," Drama Review 19 (June 1975), 129-131.

12. Ronny G. Davis, The San Francisco Mime Troupe (Palo Alto, Calif.: Ramparts Press, 1975).

13. Adrian Vargas, ed., Chicano Theatre 3 (spring 1974).

14. Lesnick, pp. 29-127.

15. Ibid., pp. 383-407.

16. Taylor, pp. 251-269.

17. Lesnick, p. 12.

18. Peter Brook, The Empty Space (London: MacGibbon and Kee, 1968), pp. 9-12.

19. Brook, p. 40.

20. Oscar G. Brockett and Robert R. Findlay, Century of Innovation (Englewood Cliffs, N.J.: Prentice-Hall, 1973), p. 780.

21. Lise Vogel, "Fine Arts and Feminism," Feminist Studies 2 (1974), 25.

22. Kate Millett, Sexual Politics (New York: Doubleday, 1969), p. 43.

23. Joelynn Snyder-Ott, "The Female Experience and Artistic Creativity," Art Education 27 (September 1974), 15.

24. Gloria Orenstein, "Art History," Signs 1 (winter 1975), 520-521.

25. Orenstein, 513.

26. Ibid., 522.

27. Kirsten Grimstad and Susan Rennie, eds., The New Woman's Survival Catalog (New York: Coward, McCann & Geoghegan, 1973), p. 139.

28. Cheri Register, "American Feminist Literary Criticism," in Feminist Literary Criticism, ed. by Josephine Donovan (Lexington: University Press of Kentucky, 1975), p. 2.

29. A Documentary Herstory of Women Artists in Revolution, 2d ed. (New York: KNOW, Inc., 1973), pp. 1-2.

30. Barbara Deckard, The Women's Movement (New York: Harper & Row, 1975), p. 430.

31. Joanna Russ, interview, Boulder, Colo., July 30, 1977.

32. Megan Terry, interview, Omaha, July 22, 1977.

33. "Theatre without Compromise and Sexism," Mademoiselle, August 1972, 288-289.

34. Margaret Croyden, "Women Directors and Playwrights," Viva, May 1974, 39.

35. Available from Women's Caucus of the Dramatists Guild, Inc.; 234 W 44th St; New York NY 10036.

36. R.G. Davis, p. 213.

37. Deckard, p. 339.

38. Sainer, The Radical Theatre Notebook, pp. 17-18.

39. Joseph Chaikin, The Presence of the Actor (New York: Atheneum, 1972), pp. 1-26.

40. Terry, interview.

41. Charles W. Ferguson, The Male Attitude (Boston: Little, Brown, 1966), p. 266.

42. Taylor, pp. 325-326.

43. Martha Boesing, interview, Minneapolis, July 18, 1977.

44. Laurie Johnson, "Sexism in the Theatre Can Be a Boon," New York Times, February 6, 1973, p. 26.

45. Webster's Seventh New Collegiate Dictionary. (Springfield, Mass.: G.& C.Merriam, 1970).

46. Joyce Indelicato, interview, Minneapolis, July 19 1977.

47. Webster's Seventh New Collegiate Dictionary.

48. Russ, interview.

49. Nancy Reeves, Womankind (Chicago: Aldine-Atherton, 1971), p. 29.

50. Judy Chicago, Through the Flower (New York: Doubleday, 1975), pp. 130-131.

51. Ibid., p. 116.

52. Ibid., p. 123.

53. Boesing, interview.

54. Russ, interview.

55. Terry, interview.

56. Linda Walsh Jenkins, ed., "Feminist Theatre News," Women in Performing Arts, April 1977, pp. 3-4.

57. Chicago, p. 116.

58. Ibid., p. 158.

59. Pat Mainardi, cited by Lise Vogel, "Fine Arts and Feminism," Feminist Studies 2 (1974), 24.

60. Ibid., 23.

61. Cindy Nemser, "Towards a Feminist Sensibility: Contemporary Trends in Women's Art," Feminist Art Journal 5 (summer 1976), 23.

62. Ibid., 21.

63. Ibid., 23.

64. Terry, interview.

65. Ibid.

66. Boesing, interview.

67. Terry, interview.

68. Ibid.

69. Boesing, interview.

70. Ibid.

71. Sally Ordway, "Feminist Theatre Playwright's Questionnaire."

72. Russ, interview.

73. Michelene Wandor, "Feminist Theatre Playwright's Questionnaire."

74. Ibid.

75. Myrna Lamb, "Feminist Theatre Playwright's Questionnaire."

76. Ibid.

77. Honor Moore, "Introduction," The New Women's Theatre (New York: Vintage Books, 1977), pp. xxix-xxxiv.

78. Martha Boesing, quoted by Eleanor Vincent, Minnesota Daily, November 14, 1975.

79. Karlyn Kohrs Campbell, "The Rhetoric of Women's Liberation: An Oxymoron," Quarterly Journal of Speech 59 (February 1975), 74-86.

80. Pattie P. Gillespie, "Feminist Theatre of the 1970's" (paper presented at the 41st annual convention of the American Theatre Association, Chicago, August 1977), p. 4.

81. Boesing, interview.

82. Moore, p. xxxiv.

83. Ibid., p. xxxvii.

84. Carol Grosberg, quoted by Karla Jay, "Carol Grosberg on Lesbian Theatre," Win 11 (June 26, 1975), 17.

85. Leonard Berkman, personal letter, September 8, 1977.

86. Charlotte Rea, "Women's Theatre Groups," Drama Review 16 (June 1972), 79-89.

87. Anselma dell'Olio, "The Founding of the New Feminist Theatre," in Notes from the Second Year, ed. by Shulamith Firestone (New York: New York Radical Feminists, 1970), p. 101.

88. Rea, "Women's Theatre Groups," 80.

89. Ibid., 82.

90. Ibid.

91. Rea, "Women's Theatre Groups," 84.

92. Linda Killian, "Westbeth," Chronicle (Hempstead, N.Y., April 5, 1973.

93. Rea, "Women's Theatre Groups," 88.

94. Ibid.

95. Mary Ann Fraulo, "W.A.F.T.: What's a Feminist Theatre?" Forecast FM 10 (1974), 46-47.

96. W.A.F.T. Newsletter 1 (spring 1975), 6.

97. Ibid., 1-5.

98. Rea, "Women's Theatre Groups," 89.

99. Chicago, Through the Flower, p. 183.

100. Killian, p. 12.

101. Lillian Perinciolo, "Feminist Theatre: They're Playing in Peoria," Ms., October 1975, 101-104.

102. W.A.F.T. Clearinghouse Bulletin 2 (spring 1975), 1.

103. Jenkins, pp. 2-4.

104. Cynthia Navaretta, "A Guide to All the Arts," Ms., December 1977, 89-90.

Chapter II

1. The Alive and Trucking Company, Stage Left (Minneapolis: By the Company, 1973), p. 1.

2. For a brief period in 1972, the members attempted to change their name to the Mill City Factory Theatre because they thought A & T might be obscure and because they planned to inhabit an abandoned factory. But since their name and reputation had been established in their first year, audiences refused to adopt the new title.

3. Meri Golden, interview, Minneapolis, July 20, 1977.

4. Stage Left, p. 3.

5. Golden, interview.

6. Stage Left, pp. 157-160.

7. Ibid., p. 2.

8. Ibid., p. 1.

9. Golden, interview.

10. Stage Left, pp. 157-160.

11. For a brief period in 1975, a black male actor worked with the group.

12. Jan Mandell, interview, Minneapolis, July 19, 1977.

13. Stage Left, p. 1.

14. Ibid., p. 2.

15. Meri Golden, "Feminst Theatre Group Questionnaire."

16. Meri Golden, "Resistance and Renewal: Alive and Trucking Theatre Co.," Common Ground, fall 1975, p. 10.

17. Ibid.

18. Mandell, interview.

19. Ibid.

20. Golden, "Resistance and Renewal," p. 10.

21. Stage Left, p. 153.

22. Ibid.

23. Carlos Morton, "The Teatro Campesino," Drama Review 18 (December 1974), 71-75.

24. Françoise Kourilsky and Leonora Champagne, "Political Theatre in France Since 1968," Drama Review 19 (June 1975), 45.

25. Golden, interview.

26. Ibid.

27. Mandell, interview.

28. Golden, Questionnaire.

29. Ibid.

30. Golden, "Resistance and Renewal," p. 8.

31. David O'Fallon, "The Maturing Theatre of Struggle," North Country Anvil, fall 1974, 62-63.

32. Stage Left, p. 154.

33. Mandell, interview.

34. Golden, "Resistance and Renewal," p. 9.

35. Golden, Questionnaire.

36. Mandell, interview.
37. Stage Left, p. 2.
38. Golden, "Resistance and Renewal," p. 10.
39. Videotapes of The People Are a River and Battered Homes and Gardens are on file at the University of Minnesota's Video Access Center in Minneapolis.
40. Review, Minneapolis Labor Review, June 22, 1972.
41. Golden, interview.
42. The Alive and Trucking Theatre Company, "The Welfare Wizard of Ours," in Stage Left (Minneapolis: By the Company, 1973), pp. 135-145.
43. Ann Payson, "Trucking Presents Brechtian Warning," Minneapolis Star, September 16, 1973.
44. Peggy Brown, review, The Paper, Model City Community Center (Minneapolis), February 20, 1974.
45. Mandell, interview.
46. Peter Vaughn, "Politics Makes Theatre Alive," Minneapolis Star, November 17, 1975.
47. Vaughn, "Politics Makes Theatre Alive."
48. Golden, interview.
49. Ibid.
50. The Alive and Trucking Theatre Company, Clown Wanted (pamphlet).
51. Mandell, interview.
52. Golden, interview.
53. Golden, Questionnaire.
54. Mandell, interview.
55. Golden, Questionnaire.
56. Walt McCaslin, review, Dayton Journal Herald, April 22, 1974.
57. Review, Minneapolis Labor Review, June 22, 1972.
58. Stage Left, p. 135.
59. McCaslin, review.
60. Golden, Questionnaire.
61. Mandell, interview.
62. Golden, interview.
63. Ibid.
64. Mandell, interview.
65. Ibid.
66. Golden, interview.
67. Page numbers refer to Stage Left.
68. Mandell, interview.
69. Schechner, Environmental Theatre, p. 251.
70. Charlotte Rea, "Women for Women," Drama Review 18 (December 1974), 79-80.
71. Mandell, interview.
72. Ibid.
73. Ibid.

74. Peter Altman, review, Minneapolis Star, February 25, 1974.

75. Golden, interview.

76. The Alive and Trucking Theatre Company, Battered Homes and Gardens, Minneapolis, 1974, p. 29. (Typewritten.)

77. Altman, review.

78. Ibid.

79. Mandell, interview.

80. Altman, review.

81. Mandell, interview.

82. McCaslin, review.

83. Mandell, interview.

Chapter III

1. Radicalesbians, "The Woman Identified Woman," in Liberation Now, ed. by Deborah Babcox and Madeline Belken (New York: Dell, 1971), p. 288.

2. Barbara Deckard, The Women's Movement: Political, Socioeconomic, and Psychological Issues (New York: Harper & Row, 1975), p. 357.

3. Ibid., 360-361.

4. The Lavender Cellar Theatre (Marie Kent, Karen Hanson and Nythar Sheehy), interview, Minneapolis, July 17, 1977. Unless otherwise credited, quoted remarks and other specific information in this chapter are from this interview. Ms. Hanson (a pseudonym) has asked that her real name not be used.

5. "Nature and Needs of the Lavender Cellar Theatre," 1974. (Mimeographed.)

6. Ibid.

7. Pat Suncircle, Cory, Minneapolis, 1974. (Typewritten.)

8. Page numbers are to Cory.

9. Marie Kent, Personal letter, September 17, 1977.

10. Michael Kirby, "On Political Theatre," Drama Review 19 (June 1975), 135.

Chapter IV

1. Circle of the Witch, "Theatre History," 1977. (Mimeographed.)

2. Circle of the Witch, Brochure, 1973.

3. Joyce Indelicato, interview, Minneapolis, July 19, 1977.

4. Circle of the Witch, "Theatre Biography," 1975. (Mimeographed.)

5.   Indelicato, interview.
6.   Gail Irish and Joyce Indelicato, "United We Act, Divided We Stall," Circle of the Witch Newsletter, summer 1977, p. 2.
7.   Micki Massimino, "Collectively Speaking," Gold Flower 5 (May-June 1977), 6.
8.   Ibid.
9.   Indelicato, interview.
10.   Rhode Island Feminist Theatre, "Feminist Theatre Group Questionnaire."
11.   Martha Boesing, interview, Minneapolis, July 18, 1977.
12.   Circle of the Witch, "Theatre History."
13.   Circle of the Witch, Brochure, 1975.
14.   Circle of the Witch, "Theatre History."
15.   Indelicato, interview.
16.   Irish and Indelicato, "United We Act, Divided We Stall," p. 2.
17.   Nancy Sugarman, interview, Minneapolis, July 19, 1977.
18.   Indelicato, interview.
19.   Ibid.
20.   Circle of the Witch, "Theatre Resume," May 1977. (Mineographed.)
21.   Indelicato, interview.
22.   Sugarman, interview.
23.   Indelicato, interview.
24.   Circle of the Witch, "Theatre History."
25.   Circle of the Witch, Sexpot Follies, 1974, p. 15. (Typewritten.)
26.   Sugarman, interview.
27.   Micki Massimino. "Collectively Speaking," p. 6.
28.   Sugarman, interview.
29.   Nancy Sugarman, "Circle of the Witch," Gold Flower 5 (March-April 1977), 6.
30.   Carlos Morton, "Sugarcoated Socialism," Drama Review 19 (June 1975), 61-68.
31.   Sugarman, interview.
32.   Ibid.
33.   Circle of the Witch, "Theatre History."
34.   Indelicato, interview.
35.   Paul Mordorski, review, Chronicle (Minneapolis), March 25, 1975.
36.   Letter to the Editor, Chronicle (Minneapolis), March 31, 1975.
37.   Roy M. Close, review, Minneapolis Star, January 28, 1975.
38.   Linda Picone, review, Minneapolis Tribune, November 16, 1975.

39. Deborah Hertz, review, <u>Common Ground</u>, winter-spring 1975, 47.

40. Marlin L. Heise, review, <u>Community Reporter</u> (St. Paul), May 1977.

41. David Raether, review, <u>Augsburg College Echo</u> (Minneapolis), March 9, 1977.

42. Sugarman, interview.

43. <u>Ibid</u>.

44. <u>Letter to Circle of the Witch, 1975.

45. Susie Klein, letter to Circle of the Witch, March 18, 1977.

46. Evelyn Bergman, letter to Circle of the Witch, June 30, 1977.

47. Indelicato, interview.

48. <u>Ibid</u>.

49. <u>Sugarman, interview.

50. Nancy Sugarman, personal letter, September 26, 1977.

Chapter V

1. At the Foot of the Mountain, "Company Resumes," 1976. (Mimeographed.)

2. Phyllis Jane Wagner, interview, Minneapolis, July 18, 1977.

3. <u>Ibid</u>.

4. <u>Martha Boesing, interview, Minneapolis, July 18, 1977.

5. <u>Ibid</u>.

6. <u>Ibid</u>.

7. <u>Martha Boesing. "Theatre of the Patriarch Versus Feminist Theatre," lecture delivered at Maidenrock Women's Learning Institute, Maidenrock, Wis., February 1977.

8. Wagner, interview.

9. Boesing, interview.

10. <u>Ibid</u>.

11. <u>Ibid</u>.

12. <u>At the Foot of the Mountain, <u>"The Moon Tree</u> Brochure," spring 1977.

13. Boesing, interview.

14. <u>Ibid</u>.

15. <u>Wagner, interview.

16. <u>Ibid</u>.

17. <u>Boesing, interview.

18. Wagner, interview.

19. Martha Boesing, "Notes on a Woman's Process for Creating a Theatre Event," in <u>Women in Performing Arts</u>, ed. by Linda Walsh Jenkins, April 1977, p. 3.

20. Boesing, interview.
21. At the Foot of the Mountain, "The Moon Tree Brochure," spring 1977.
22. Wagner, interview.
23. Martha Boesing, River Journal, 1975, p. 8. (Unpublished.)
24. Lisa Henrickson, review, Minnesota Daily, November 26, 1975.
25. Page numbers are to River Journal.
26. Kathy Frank Chesney, review, Gold Flower 4 (February 1976).
27. Mary Ellen Shaw, review, Many Corners, December 1975, 15.
28. Henrickson, review.
29. Eleanor Vincent, Minnesota Daily, November 14, 1975.
30. Martha Boesing, Introduction to The Moon Tree, 1977, p. i. (Unpublished.) Page numbers are to Moon Tree.
31. Boesing, interview.
32. Wagner, interview.
33. Shaw, review.
34. Henrickson, review.
35. Roy M. Close, review, Minneapolis Star, July 12, 1976.
36. Arthur Sainer, review, Village Voice, November 22, 1976.
37. Wagner, interview.
38. Sainer, review.
39. Phyllis Jane Wagner, "Introduction," Journeys Along the Matrix: Three Plays by Martha Boesing (Minneapolis: Vanilla Press, 1978), pp. 9-10.
40. Boesing, interview.

Chapter VI

1. Morgan Y. Himelstein, Drama Was a Weapon (New Brunswick, N.J.: Rutgers University Press, 1963), p. 3.
2. Ibid., p. 13.
3. Harold Clurman, The Fervent Years (New York: Hill and Wang, 1957), pp. 138-143.
4. Himelstein, pp. 37-51.
5. Ibid., p. 232.
6. Hallie Flanagan, Arena (New York: B. Blom, 1940).
7. Himelstein, pp. 111-112.
8. In 1977 feminist theatre and the Federal Theatre merged in a new play, Women's Drama of the 1930's, presented by the New Federal Theatre. Primarily composed of

cuttings from FTP plays and dramatized events in Hallie
Flanagan's career, the play reveals a range of 1930's views
of women.

9. Edith J.R. Isaacs, The Negro in the American
Theatre (New York: Theatre Arts, 1947), pp. 121-122.

10. Larry Neal, "The Black Arts Movement," Drama
Review 12 (summer 1968), 39.

11. Margaret Wilkerson, "Black Theatre in California," Drama Review 16 (December 1972), 29.

12. Neal, "Black Arts Movement," p. 33.

13. Dolores Brandon, letter, The Women's Salon
[newsletter], summer 1977, p. 3.

14. Neal, "Black Art Movement," p. 29.

15. Victoria Sullivan and James Hatch eds., "Introduction," Plays by and about Women (New York: Vintage
Books, 1974), p. vii.

16. Wilkerson, "Black Theatre in California," 50-51.

17. Adam David Miller, "It's a Long Way to St.
Louis," Drama Review 12 (summer, 1968), 149.

18. Jessica B. Harris, "The National Black Theatre,"
Drama Review 16 (December 1972), 40.

19. Wilkerson, "Black Theatre in California," 31-32.

20. Harris, "National Black Theatre," 40.

21. Lisbeth Grant, "The New Lafayette Theatre,"
Drama Review 16 (December 1972), 50-51.

22. Barbara Deckard, The Women's Movement: Political, Socioeconomic, and Psychological Issues (New York:
Harper & Row, 1975), pp. 361-362, 363.

Chapter VII

1. Pattie P. Gillespie, "Feminist Theatre of the
1970's" (paper presented at the 41st annual convention of
the American Theatre Association, Chicago, August 1977),
pp. 5-6.

2. Deborah Fortson, Feminist Theatre Playwright's
Questionnaire.

3. Joanna Russ, "Why Women Can't Write," in
Images of Women in Fiction, ed. by Susan Koppelman
Cornillon (Bowling Green, Ohio: Bowling Green University
Popular Press, 1972), p. 19.

4. Gloria Orenstein, "Art History," Signs 1 (winter
1975), 516-517.

5. Roberta Sklar, quoted by Charlotte Rea, "Women
for Women," Drama Review 18 (December 1974), 84-85.

6. Karen Malpede, Letter, The Women's Salon [news-
letter], summer 1977, p. 4.

7. Orenstein, "Art History," 520.

8. Megan Terry, interview, Omaha, July 22, 1977.

9. Myrna Lamb, Feminist Theatre Playwright's Questionnaire.

10. Michelene Wandor, Feminist Theatre Playwright's Questionnaire.

11. Terry, interview.

12. Joanna Russ, interview, Boulder, Colo., July 30, 1977.

13. Virginia Woolf, A Room of One's Own (New York: Harcourt, Brace & World, 1929), p. 80.

14. Russ, "Why Women Can't Write," pp. 12-16.

15. Honor Moore, "Theatre Will Never Be the Same," Ms., (December, 1977), p. 74.

16. Woolf, A Room of One's Own, pp. 68-69.

17. Ibid., p. 79.

18. See Mary Ellman, Thinking About Women (New York: Harcourt Brace Jovanovich, 1968); Jean Elizabeth Gagen, The New Woman: Her Emergence in English Drama 1600-1730 (New York: Twayne, 1954); Vivian Gornick and Barbara K. Morgan, eds., Woman in Sexist Society (New York: Basic Books, 1971); Kate Millet, Sexual Politics (New York: Doubleday, 1969); and Virginia Woolf, A Room of One's Own.

19. Gillespie, "Feminist Theatre of the 1970's," p. 5.

20. Lucy Winer, quoted by Charlotte Rea, "Women for Women," Drama Review 18 (December 1974), 87.

21. Russ, "Why Women Can't Write," p. 6.

22. Carol Grosberg, quoted by Karla Jay, "Carol Grosberg on Lesbian Theatre," Win 11 (June 26, 1975), 17.

23. At the Foot of the Mountain Newsletter, November, 1977. (Mimeographed.)

24. Russ, "Why Women Can't Write," p. 4.

25. Ibid. pp. 15-16.

26. Jane Ellen Harrison, Ancient Art and Ritual (New York: Henry Holt, 1913), p. 41.

27. Cynthia Navaretta, "A Guide to All the Arts," Ms., December 1977, 87-90.

28. Meri Golden, interview, Minneapolis, July 20, 1977.

29. Martha Boesing, interview, Minneapolis, July 18, 1977.

30. Barbara Field, telephone conversation, Minneapolis, July 21, 1977.

31. Emily Mann, telephone conversation, Minneapolis, July 21, 1977.

32. Gillespie, "Feminist Theatre of the 1970's," p. 4.

33. Ibid.

34. Boesing, interview.

35. Ibid.

36. Orenstein, "Art History," 521.
37. Nancy Sugarman, interview, Minneapolis, July 19, 1977.
38. Boesing, interview.
39. Marilyn Stasio, "The Nights the Critics Lost Their Cool," Ms., Spetember 1975, 37-41.
40. Margaret Lamb, "Feminist Criticism," Drama Review 18 (Spetember 1974), 50.
41. Karen Malpede, personal letter, September 24, 1977.
42. Russ, "Why Women Can't Write," p. 20.
43. Albert Camus, The Rebel (New York: Knopf, 1974), p. 13.
44. Ibid., p. 14.

BIBLIOGRAPHY

(See also Chapter Notes; List of Plays Cited)

Books

Biner, Pierre. The Living Theatre. New York: Horizon Press, 1972.

Brockett, Oscar G., and Robert R. Findlay. Century of Innovation. Englewood Cliffs, N.J.: Prentice-Hall, 1973.

Brook, Peter. The Empty Space. London: MacGibbon & Kee, 1968.

Brown, Janet. Feminist Drama: Definition and Critical Analysis. Metuchen, N.J.: Scarecrow Press, 1980.

Camus, Albert. The Rebel. New York: Knopf, 1974.

Chaikin, Joseph. The Presence of the Actor. New York: Atheneum, 1972.

Chicago, Judy. Through the Flower. New York: Doubleday, 1975.

Clurman, Harold. The Fervent Years. New York: Hill and Wang, 1957.

Davis, R.G. The San Francisco Mime Troupe. Palo Alto, Calif.: Ramparts Press, 1975.

Deckard, Barbara. The Women's Movement: Political, Socioeconomic, and Psychological Issues. New York: Harper & Row, 1975.

A Documentary Herstory of Women Artists in Revolution, 2d ed. New York: KNOW, Inc., 1973.

Ellman, Mary. Thinking About Women. New York: Harcourt Brace Jovanovich, 1968.

124

Ferguson, Charles W. The Male Attitude. Boston: Little, Brown, 1966.

Flanagan, Hallie. Arena. New York: B. Blom, 1940.

France, Rachel. A Century of Plays by American Women. New York: Richards Rosen Press, 1979.

Gagen, Jean Elizabeth. The New Woman: Her Emergence in English Drama 1600-1730. New York: Twayne, 1954.

Gornick, Vivian, and Barbara K. Morgan, eds. Woman in Sexist Society: Studies in Power and Powerlessness. New York: Basic Books, 1971.

Grimstad, Kirsten, and Susan Rennie, eds. The New Woman's Survival Catalog. New York: Coward, McCann & Geoghegan, 1973.

Harrison, Jane Ellen. Ancient Art and Ritual. New York: Henry Holt, 1913.

Haskell, Molly. From Reverence to Rape. New York: Holt, Rinehart & Winston, 1974.

Himelstein, Morgan Y. Drama Was a Weapon: The Left-Wing Theatre in New York 1929-1941. New Brunswick, N.J.: Rutgers University Press, 1963.

Hope, Diane S. A Rhetorical Definition of Movements: The Drama of Rebirth in Radical Feminism. Dissertation. Buffalo: State University of New York, 1975.

Hotchkiss, Marlow. Firehouse Theatre. Minneapolis: By the Author, 1969.

Isaacs, Edith J.R. The Negro in the American Theatre. New York: Theatre Arts, 1947.

Lamb, Myrna. The Mod Donna and Scyklon Z. New York: Pathfinder Press, 1971.

Lesnick, Henry, ed. Guerilla Street Theatre. New York: Avon Books, 1973.

Lippard, Lucy R. From the Center: Feminist Essays on Women's Art. New York: E.P. Dutton, 1976.

Millett, Kate. Sexual Politics. New York: Doubleday, 1969.

Moore, Honor. The New Women's Theatre. New York: Vintage Books, 1977.

Morgan, Robin, ed. Sisterhood Is Powerful. New York: Random House, 1970.

Pasolli, Robert. A Book on the Open Theatre. Indianapolis: Bobbs-Merrill, 1970.

Rabkin, Gerald. Drama and Commitment: Politics in American Theatre of the Thirties. Bloomington: Indiana University Press, 1964.

Reeves, Nancy. Womankind. Chicago: Aldine-Atherton, 1971.

Sainer, Arthur. The Radical Theatre Notebook. New York: Avon Books, 1975.

Schechner, Richard. Environmental Theatre. New York: Hawthorne Books, 1973.

Spacks, Patricia Meyer. The Female Imagination. New York: Knopf, 1975.

Sullivan, Victoria, and James Hatch, eds. Plays by and about Women. New York: Vintage Books, 1974.

Taylor, Karen Malpede. People's Theatre in Amerika. New York: Drama Book Specialists/Publishers, 1972.

Wagner, Phyllis Jane. Megan Terry: Political Playwright. Dissertation. Denver: University of Denver, 1975.

Woolf, Virginia. A Room of One's Own. New York: Harcourt, Brace & World, 1929.

Zastrow, Sylvia V.A. The Structure of Selected Plays by American Women Playwrights 1920-1970. Dissertation. Evanston, Ill.: Northwestern University, 1975.

Articles

Allegra, Donna. "Hot Doo-Wop Meets Too Cool to Care." Majority Report, February 18-March 3, 1978, 7.

Ball, Aimee Lee, and Frances Ruffin. "Applause! Women in the Arts." Redbook, September 1977, 37-44.

Boesing, Martha. "Notes on a Woman's Process for Creating a Theatre Event." In Women in Performing Arts, edited by Linda Walsh Jenkins (April 1977), 1-6.

Brandon, Dolores. Letter. The Women's Salon [Newsletter], summer, 1977, 1-4.

Brock, H. "Women in Modern Drama." Intellect, May 1977, 388.

Brown, Janet Patricia. "Kenneth Burke and the Mod Donna: The Dramatistic Method Applied to Feminist Criticism." Central States Speech Journal, summer 1978, 138-144.

Campbell, Karlyn Kohrs. "The Rhetoric of Women's Liberation: An Oxymoron." Quarterly Journal of Speech 59 (February 1975), 74-86.

Castedo-Ellerman, Elena. "Feminism or Femineity? Six Women Writers Answer." Américas, October 1978, 19-24.

Chesney, Kathy Frank. Review. Gold Flower 4 (February 1976).

Croyden, Margaret. "Women Directors and Playwrights." Viva, May 1974, 39-40.

Curb, Rosemary. "The First Decade of Feminist Theatre in America" (mimeographed). Available from the aurthor c/o Dept. of English, Rollins College, Winter Park FL 32789.

Datson, Marijane, ed. The Women in Theatre Newsletter (fall, 1978). P.O. Box 9161, Santa Rosa CA 95402.

dell'Olio, Anselma. "The Founding of the New Feminist Theatre." In Notes from the Second Year: Women's Liberation--Major Writings of the Radical Feminists, edited by Shulamith Firestone (New York: New York Radical Feminists, 1970), 101-102.

Drexler, Rosalyn. "The New Androgyny," Vogue, February 1977, 94.

Dworkin, Susan.   "The Gall of Ivy."   Ms., November 1976,
     31-32.

_____.   "Nightclub Cantata: A   Soundtrack   for
     Emotions."   Ms., June 1977, 18-22.

Epstein, Renee.   "The Club: A Musical Double Take in
     Drag."   Ms., March 1977, 34-36.

Fraulo, Mary Ann.   "W.A.F.T.:   What's a Feminist The-
     atre?"   Forecast FM 10 (1974), 46-47.

Freeman, Alexa, and Jackie MacMillan.   "Prime Time: Art
     and Politics."   Quest, fall 1975, 27-39.

Gelderman,   Carol   W.   "The   Male   Nature   of   Tragedy."
     Prairie Schooner, fall 1975, 220-236.

Gillespie, Patti P.   "Feminist Theatre: A Rhetorical Phen-
     omenon."   Quarterly Journal of Speech, October 1978,
     284-294.

_____.   "Listing of Feminist Theatres."   Theatre
     News, November 1977, 22-24.

Golden, Meri.   "Resistance and Renewal: Alive and Truck-
     ing   Theatre   Company."   Common Ground, fall 1975,
     8-10.

Gottlieb,   Lois   C.   "Obstacles   to   Feminism   in   the   Early
     Plays   of   Rachel   Crothers."   University of Michigan
     Papers in Women's Studies, June 1975, 71-84.

Gould, Lois.   "Who Is Eva Perón and Why Has She Come
     Back Singing?"   Ms., September 1979, 28-34.

Goulianos,   Joan.   "Women   in   the   Avant-Garde   Theatre."
     In Women: An Issue, edited by Lee Edwards, Mary
     Heath   and   Lisa   Baskin   (Boston: Little,   Brown,
     1972), p. 257-267.

Grant, Lisbeth.   "The   New   Lafayette   Theatre."   Drama
     Review 16 (December 1972), 46-55.

Harris, Jessica B.   "The National Black Theatre."   Drama
     Review, 19 (December 1972), 39-45.

Hertz, Deborah.   Review.   Common Ground, winter-spring
     1975, 46-47.

Irish, Gail, and Joyce Indelicato. "United We Act, Div-
    ided We Stall." Circle of the Witch Newsletter 1
    (summer 1977), 1-10.

"It's Happening ... in New Haven, L.A., New York." Ms.,
    June 1978, 26-32.

Jay, Karla. "Carol Grosberg on Lesbian Theatre." Win
    11 (June 26, 1975), 15-17.

Jenkins, Linda Walsh, ed. "Feminist Theatre News." In
    Women in Performing Arts (April 1977), 1-6.

_____. "Women in Theatre Today." Theatre
    News, November 1977, 4.

Kalem, T.E. "The Faces of Eve." Time, March 1972.

Kirby, Michael. "On Political Theatre." Drama Review 19
    (June 1975), 129-135.

Kourilsky, Françoise, and Leonora Champagne. "Political
    Theatre in France Since 1968." Drama Review 19
    (June 1975), 43-52.

Lamb, Margaret. "Feminist Criticism." Drama Review 18
    (September 1974), 46-50.

The Lavender Cellar Theatre. "Nature and Needs of the
    Lavender Cellar Theatre" (mineographed.) Minne-
    apolis, 1974.

Lewis, Barbara. "What's $80,000. Split 35 Ways?" Ms.,
    May 1979, 71-72.

Lynd, Phyllis. "That's a Heavy Crown Mr. Jones." Fem-
    inist Art Journal, winter 1976-77, 30-32.

Massimino, Micki. "Collectively Speaking" Gold Flower 5
    (May-June 1977), 6-7.

Miller, Adam David. "It's a Long Way to St. Louis." Dra-
    ma Review 12 (summer 1968), 147-150.

Moore, Honor. "Can You Talk About Your Mother Without
    Crying?" Ms., November 1977, 29-30.

_____. "Theatre Will Never Be the Same." Ms.,
    December 1977, 36-75.

Morton, Carlos. "Sugarcoated Socialism." Drama Review 19 (June 1975), 61-68.

_____. "The Teatro Campesino." Drama Review 18 (December 1974), 71-76.

Navaretta, Cynthia. "A Guide to All the Arts." Ms. December 1977, 87-90.

Neal, Larry. "The Black Arts Movement." Drama Review 12 (summer 1968), 29-39.

Nemser, Cindy. "Towards a Feminist Sensibility: Contemporary Trends in Women's Art." Feminist Art Journal 5 (summer 1976), 19-23.

Newman, Phyllis. "On Being 'The Madwoman of Central Park West'." Ms., May 1979, 41-42.

O'Fallon, David. "The Maturing Theatre of Struggle." North Country Anvil, fall 1974. 62-63.

Orenstein, Gloria. "Art History." Signs 1 (winter 1975), 505-525.

Ozick, Cynthia. "Does Genius Have a Gender?" Ms., December 1977, 56.

Perinciolo, Lillian. "Feminist Theatre: They're Playing in Peoria." Ms., October 1975, 101-104.

Pogrebin, Letty Cottin. "'Yentl': Better a Fool Than a Woman." Ms., February 1976, 37-39.

Radicalesbians. "The Woman Identified Woman." In Liberation Now, edited by Deborah Babcox and Madeline Belken (New York: Dell, 1971).

Rea, Charlotte. "Women for Women." Drama Review 18 (December 1974), 77-87.

_____. "Women's Theatre Groups." Drama Review 16 (June 1972), 79-89.

Register, Cheri. "American Feminist Literary Criticism: A Bibliographical Introduction." In Feminist Literary Criticism, edited by Josephine Donovan (Lexington: University Press of Kentucky, 1975).

Russ, Joanna. "What Can a Heroine Do? or Why Women Can't Write," In Images of Women in Fiction: Feminist Perspectives, edited by Susan Koppleman Cornillon (Bowling Green, Ohio: Bowling Green University Popular Press, 1972).

Shange, Ntozake. "Ntozake Shange Interviews Herself." Ms., December 1977, 40-45.

Shaw, Mary Ellen. Review. Many Corners, December 1975, 15.

Snyder-Ott, Joelynn. "The Female Experience and Artistic Creativity." Art Education 27 (September 1974), 15-18.

Stasio, Marilyn. "The Nights the Critics Lost Their Cool." Ms., September 1975, 37-41.

Stone, Laurie. "Sister/Sister--Working It Out on Stage." Ms., November 1978, 40-45.

Sugarman, Nancy. "Circle of the Witch." Gold Flower 5 (March-April 1977), 6-7.

Sullivan, Ruth. "Big Mama, Big Papa, and Little Sons in Ken Kesey's 'One Flew Over the Cuckoo's Nest'." Literature and Psychology 25 (1975) 34-44.

"Theatre without Compromise and Sexism." Mademoiselle, August 1972, 288-387.

Vargas, Adrian, ed. Chicano Theatre 3 (spring 1974).

Vogel, Lise. "Fine Arts and Feminism." Feminist Studies (1974).

Wagner, Phyllis Jane. "Introduction." In Journeys Along the Matrix: Three plays by Martha Boesing (Minneapolis: Vanilla Press, 1977).

Weinstein, Joyce, and Isabel Bishop. "Forum: Are Women Artists Discriminated Against?" American Artist, May 1978, 18-19.

Wilkerson, Margaret. "The Black Theatre in California." Drama Review 16 (December 1972), 25-38.

Wolfe, Ruth. "The Aesthetics of Violence: Women Tackle the Rough Stuff." Ms., February 1979, 30-36.

Newspapers

Chronicle [Hempstead, N.Y.]. April 5, 1973.

Chronicle [Minneapolis]. March 25 and 31 , 1975.

Community Reporter [St. Paul]. May, 1977.

Dayton Journal Herald. Review. April 22, 1974.

Echo [Minneapolis]. Review. March 9, 1977.

Gussow, Mel. "Theatre: Women's Work: Cutting Edge's
     Croon at Performing Garage." New York Times,
     March 30, 1976, 39.

Minneapolis Labor Review. Review. June 22, 1972.

Minneapolis Star. Reviews. September 16, 1973, Febru-
     ary 25, 1974, January 28, 1975, November 17, 1975,
     July 12, 1976.

Minneapolis Tribune. Review. November 16, 1975.

Minnesota Daily. November 14 and 26, 1975.

New York Times. February 6, 1973.

The Paper, Model City Community Center [Minneapolis].
     Review. February 20, 1974.

Village Voice. Review, November 22, 1976.

Academic Papers

Boesing, Martha. "Theatre of the Patriarch Versus Fem-
     inist Theatre." Lecture delivered at Maidenrock
     Women's Learning Institute, Maidenrock, Wis., Feb-
     ruary 1977.

Davis, Betty Moseley. "Feminist Theatre: An Identity
     Crisis." Paper delivered at the Southeastern Theatre
     Conference, Norfolk, Va., March 1977.

Gillespie, Pattie P. "Feminist Theatre of the 1970's."
     Paper presented at the 41st annual convention of the
     American Theatre Association, Chicago, August 1977.

LIST OF PLAYS CITED

The Alive and Trucking Theatre Company. Battered Homes and Gardens. Minneapolis, 1974. (Typewritten).

_____. Stage Left. Minneapolis: By the Company, 1973. Contains Pig in a Blanket, The Welfare Wizard of Ours and The People Are a River.

At the Foot of the Mountain. Raped: A Woman's Look at Brecht's Exception and the Rule. Minneapolis, 1976. (Unpublished).

_____. The Story of a Mother. Minneapolis, 1978. (Unpublished).

Boesing, Martha. Journeys Along the Matrix: Three Plays by Martha Boesing. Minneapolis: Vanilla Press, 1978. Contains The Gelding, River Journal, and Love Song for an Amazon.

_____. The Moon Tree. Minneapolis, 1977. (Typewritten.) Performed by At the Foot of the Mountain.

_____. Pimp. Minneapolis, 1973. (Typewritten.) Performed by At the Foot of the Mountain.

Brooke, Dinah, and Michelene Wandor. Sink Songs: Feminist Plays. London: Privately Published, 1975 (Michelene Wandor; 51 Belsize Lane; London, NW3, England). Contains Wandor's Mal de Mere, Joey, Christmas Pearls and Swallows and Brooke's Love Food and That's My Boy.

Circle of the Witch. The Changebringers: A Fantasy of Women and Work. Minneapolis, 1977. (Unpublished.)

_____. Lady in the Corner. Minneapolis, 1975. (Typewritten.)

_____. Sexpot Follies. Minneapolis, 1974. (Type-
written.)

_____. Time Is Passing. Minneapolis, 1976.
(Typewritten.)

The Co-Respondents. Give Em an Inch. (Unpublished.)

_____. Here She Comes. (Unpublished.)

Fortson, Deborah. Baggage. Cambridge, 1975. (Typewritten.) Performed by the Commonplace Pageant.

_____. Mermaids. Cambridge, 1977. (Unpub-
lished.) Performed by the Commonplace Pageant.

Geoffrey, Marisa. Bread and Roses. Contact New Feminist Talent, 250 57th St, New York NY 10019.

Goldsmith, Gloria. Womanspeak. Pioneer Drama Service,
P.O. Box 22555, Denver CO 80222.

Greth, Roma. President's Daughter/President's Wife. Performed by the Washington Area Feminist Theatre.

Griffin, Susan. Voices: A Play. New York: Feminist
Press, 1975.

Gunn, Gwen. Across the Street. New York, 1971. (Typewritten.) Performed by the Westbeth Playwright's
Feminist Collective.

Hansberry, Lorraine. A Raisin in the Sun. New York:
Signet Books, 1958.

Holden, Joan. The Independent Female or A Man Has His
Pride. San Francisco, 1970. In Notes from the
Third Year, 1971.

Lamb, Myrna. Plays of Women's Liberation: The Mod Donna and Scyklon Z. New York: Pathfinder Press,
1971.

_____. The Two Party System. (Unpublished.)
Performed at the Interart Theatre, New York.

Malpede, Karen. The End of the War. New York, 1977.
(Unpublished.) Performed by the New Cycle Theatre.

_____. Rebeccah. New York, 1977. (Unpub-
lished.) Performed by the Rebeccah Company.

Merriam, Eve. The Club. 1976. Available from Samuel
French.

Moore, Honor, ed. The New Women's Theatre. New York:
Vintage Books, 1977. Contains Corinne Jacker's
Bits and Pieces, Joanna Russ' Window Dressing, Ur-
sule Molinaro's Breakfast Past Noon, Tina Howe's
Birth and After Birth, Honor Moore's Mourning Pic-
tures, Alice Childress' Wedding Band, Ruth Wolff's
The Abdication, Joanna Halpert Kraus' The Ice Wolf,
Myrna Lamb's I Lost a Pair of Gloves Yesterday, and
Eve Merriam's, Paula Wagner's and Jack Hoffsiss' Out
of Our Father's House.

The New Feminist Theatre. Cabaret of Sexual Politics.
New York, 1971. (Unpublished.)

The Open Stage. Eleanor! (Unpublished.)

_____. Marie! (Unpublished.)

_____. Sisters of Liberty. (Unpublished.)

Ordway, Sally. Crabs. In Scripts I, December 1971,
p. 26. Performed by the Westbeth Playwright's Feminist Collective.

_____. There's a Wall Between Us, Darling. New
York, 1965. (Typewritten.) Performed by the Westbeth Playwright's Feminist Collective.

Rhode Island Feminist Theatre. Anne Hutchinson. 1976.
(Unpublished.)

_____. The Johnnie Show. Shubert Playbook
Series, II, 4, 1975.

_____. O Women's Piece. 1973. (Unpublished.)

_____. Persephone's Return. Shubert Playbook
Series, III, 2, 1975.

_____. Clowns of the Stars and Moon Circus.
1976. (Unpublished.)

_____. Taking It Off. Hellcoal Playbook Series,
I, 7, 1973.

Rites of Women. Rites of Passage. 1975. (Unpublished.)

_____. Rites of Torture. 1976. (Unpublished.)

_____. Womanritual. 1976. (Unpublished.)

Shange, Ntozake. For Colored Girls Who Have Considered Suicide/When the Rainbow Is Enuf. New York: Macmillan, 1976.

Sullivan, Victoria, and James Hatch, eds. Plays by and about Women. New York: Vintage Books, 1974. Contains Alice Gerstenberg's Overtones, Lillian Hellman's The Children's Hour, Clare Boothe's The Women, Doris Lessing's Play with a Tiger, Megan Terry's Calm Down Mother, Natalia Ginzburg's The Advertisement, Maureen Duffy's Rites, and Alice Childress' Wine in the Wilderness.

Suncircle, Pat. Cory. Minneapolis, 1974. (Typewritten.) Performed by the Lavender Cellar Theatre.

_____. Prisons. Minneapolis, 1973. (Unpublished.) Performed by the Lavender Cellar Theatre.

Terry, Megan. Babes in the Bighouse. (Unpublished.) Performed by At the Foot of the Mountain and the Omaha Magic Theatre.

_____. Approaching Simone. Old Westbury, N.Y.: The Feminist Press, 1973.

Walker, Dolores. Abide in Darkness. New York, 1971. (Typewritten.) Performed as part of Rape-In by the Westbeth Playwright's Feminist Collective.

Womanrite Theatre Ensemble. Daughters. New York, 1976. (Unpublished.)

Yankowitz, Susan, and the Open Theatre. Terminal. In Scripts I, 1969.

LIST OF AMERICAN
FEMINIST THEATRE GROUPS

Actor's Sorority. 1024 Norton, Kansas City MO 64127.

"Ain't I a Woman?" Theatre. Paula Sperry, c/o Woman to Woman Feminist Book Center, 2023 E Colfax, Denver CO. (303) 320-5972.

The Alive and Trucking Theatre Company. c/o Jan Mandell, 3636 Chicago Ave S, Minneapolis MN 55407. (612) 825-1910.

Artists in Prison. P.O. Box 49605, Los Angeles CA 90049.

At the Foot of the Mountain. 3144 10th Ave S, Minneapolis MN 55407. (612) 871-2101.

B & O Women's Theatre. c/o Mary Bergquist and Karen Olila, Champaign IL 61820. (217) 328-3653.

Big Mama Poetry Theatre. 1649 Coventry Road, Cleveland OH 44118. (216) 371-0441.

Black Star Theatre. Nancy Krieger, 13 Ellery St, apt 2, Cambridge MA 02138.

Boulder Feminist Theatre Collective. c/o Juliet Wittman, 7241 S Boulder Rd, Boulder CO 80302. (303)494-4535.

Bread and Roses Company. c/o New Feminist Talent, Inc. 250 W 57th St, New York NY 10026. (212) 581-1006.

Bread and Roses Theatre. 1536 Oak Grove Dr, Los Angeles CA 90041. (213) 254-3536.

The Cambridge Ensemble. Old Cambridge Baptist Church, 1151 Massachusetts Ave, Cambridge MA 02138. (617) 876-2545.

Caravan Theatre. 1555 Massachusetts Ave, Cambridge MA 02138. 617-868-8520.

Caught in the Act. Hillary Carlip, 648 Castro, San Francisco CA 94114. (415) 552-0679.

Chicago's Women's Theatre Group, Inc. Marilyn Kollath, 7100 N Greenview, Chicago IL 60626. (312) 761-7075.

Circle of the Witch. 2953 Bloomington Ave S, Minneapolis MN 55407. (612) 729-6200.

Commonplace Pageant Theatre. c/o Deborah Fortson, 41 Magnolia Rd, Cambridge MA 02138. (617) 547-1368.

The Co-Respondents. 109 E 21st St, Olympia WA 98501. (206) 866-1830.

The Cutting Edge. c/o Andrea Balis, 36 E 7th St, New York NY 10003. (212) 254-4850.

Earth Onion Women's Theatre. 2416 18th St NW, Washington DC 20010. (202) 667-3785.

Emmatroupe. 16 Waverly Pl, New York NY 10003. (212) 677-2652.

Encompass Theatre. c/o Nancy Rhodes, 168 W 48th St, New York NY 10036. (212) 575-1558.

Greenville Feminist Theatre. c/o Anne Davis, 304 Chick Springs Rd, Greenville SC 29609. (803) 233-1446.

Harrison and Tyler. c/o Harry Walker, Inc. Empire State Bldg, Suite 3616, 350 Fifth Ave, New York NY 10001.

Interart Theatre. Women's Interart Center, 549 W 52nd, New York NY 10019. (212) 246-6570.

Invisible Theatre. 1400 N First Ave, Tucson AZ 85719.

It's All Right to Be Woman Theatre. c/o Sue Perglut, 254 W 15th St, New York NY 10011.

It's Just a Stage. c/o Iris Landsberg, 214 Valencia, San Francisco CA 94103.

Las Cucarachas. Concilio Mujeres, P.O. Box 27524, San Francisco CA 94127.

Lavender Cellar Theatre. c/o Lesbian Resource Center, 2104 Stevens Ave S, Minneapolis MN 55403. (612) 871-2601.

Lesbian-Feminist Theatre Collective of Pittsburgh. c/o Ann Sadler, 421 Braddock Rd, Pittsburgh PA 15221.

Lilith Women's Theatre Collective. c/o Michele Linfaute, Box 1174, San Francisco CA 94101.

The Lion Walk Center. c/o Anne Wyma, 420 N Craig St, Pittsburgh PA 15213. (412) 422-9088.

Listeners Theatre. c/o Sharon Daily Pattison, Dept of Speech, Indiana State University, Terre Haute IN 47809.

Los Angeles Feminist Theatre. c/o Olivia B. Watt, 3464 Grandview Blvd, Los Angeles CA 90066.

Medusa's Revenge. 10 Bleecker St, New York NY. (212) 532-4151.

Mermaid Theatre. c/o Deborah Fortson, 41 Magnolia Ave, Cambridge MA 02138. (617) 547-1368.

Mischief Mime. 328 E State St, Ithaca NY 14850.

The Migrant Theatre. c/o Joanne Foreman, P.O. Box 4058, Albuquerque NM 87106.

Motion: The Women's Performing Collective. 141 Pine St, San Anselmo CA 94960. (415) 456-8165.

New Cycle Theatre. c/o Karen Malpede, 657 Fifth Ave, Brooklyn NY 11215. (212) 788-7098.

New Feminist Repertory Theatre. c/o Anselma dell'Olio, 1246 N Sweetzer Ave, Los Angeles CA 90060. (213) 656-6015.

New World Theatre. c/o Other Side of Today Shop, 135 Jay St, Schenectady NY 12309.

The New York Feminist Theatre Troupe. 157 Garfield Pl Number 3, Brooklyn NY 11215. (212) 768-2228.

The New York Tea Party. c/o Elizabeth Perry, 235 W 76th St, Suite 90, New York NY 10023. (212) 877-8134.

Nickle and Dime Productions. c/o Women's Resource Center, University Center, Missoula MT 59801.

Omaha Magic Theatre. c/o Lynn Herrick, 1417 Farnam St, Omaha NE 68102.

The Onyx Women's Theatre. c/o Sylvia Witts Vitale, 116-43 141st St, South Ozone Pk NY 11436. (212) 322-7497.

The Open Stage. 64 Canterbury Gate, Lynbrook NY 11563. (212) 593-4425.

The Orange County Feminist Theatre. 2549 Runyan Pl, Anaheim CA 92804. (714) 828-1134.

Pagoda Theatre-by-the-Sea. 207 Coastal Highway, St Augustine FL 32084. (904) 824-2970.

The People's Playhouse. c/o Kate Krebs, 94-25 57th Ave, Elmhurst NY 11373. (212) 271-6093.

Poor Sid Theatre. c/o YWCA, Madison WI 53701.

Rainbow Company. c/o Ellen Snorthand, 7247 Kester Ave, Van Nuys CA 91405. (213) 980-1242.

Rattling the Chains Theatre. c/o Barbara Cloyd, 1039 Pinegate, St. Louis MO 63122. (314) 965-1854.

Reality Theatre. P.O. Box 464, Kenmore Square Sta, Boston MA 02215.

Red Dyke Theatre. 1850 New York Ave NE, Atlanta GA 30307.

Rhode Island Feminist Theatre. Box 9083, Providence RI 02940. (401) 861-2059.

Rites of Women Lesbian Feminist Theatre. 1526 S 18th St, Philadelphia PA 19146. (215) 474-3671.

River Queen Women's Center. c/o Nola M. Dick, 17140 River Rd, P.O. Box 173, Guernewood Park CA 95446.

Sisters of Light. c/o Jackie Early, 46 Skyview Dr, Denver CO 80215.

Sisters on Stage. c/o Carol Perkins, 5009 Randlett Dr, LaMesa CA 92041. (714) 463-5290.

Spider Woman Theatre Workshop. 333 DeGraw St, Brooklyn NY 11215.

The Sunshine Company. c/o Mae Canaga, 9660 Denver St, Ventura CA 93003.

Synthaxis Theatre [Los Angeles]. 1139 B. Foothill St, South Pasadena CA 91030. (213) 441-2835.

Thank You Theatre. c/o Woman's Center, 218 S Venice Blvd, Los Angeles CA 90046.

Theatre Company of Ann Arbor. c/o Stella Mitzfud, 1101 Miner, Ann Arbor MI 48107.

Theatre of Light and Shadow. Box 620, Botsford CT 06404.

Theatre of Process. 111 E Gutierrez St, Santa Barbara CA 93101.

Uncommon Lady from Bloomsbury. c/o Sara DeWitt, 437 Whiting St, El Segundo CA 90245.

Vermont Women's Theatre. c/o Roz Payne, P.O. Box 164, Richmond VT 05477.

Walking the Tightrope: Herstory. c/o Annette Martin, Dept of Speech and Dramatic Arts, Eastern Michigan University, Ypsilanti MI 48197. (313) 487-0032.

Washington Area Feminist Theatre. 2100 Foxhall Rd NW, Washington DC 20007. (202) 965-0971.

Westbeth Playwrights Feminist Collective. 463 West St, Studio 402D, New York NY 10014.

"Who's a Lady?" Company. c/o Margaret Berger, 199 Temple St, West Newton Hill MA 02165. (617) 322-8430.

Womanrite Theatre Ensemble. c/o Karen Brukhardt, 110 W 14th St, 7th floor, New York NY. (212) 857-4653.

Woman's Collage Theatre. 15 W 17th St, New York NY 10011. (212) 924-4388.

Woman's Ensemble. P.O. Box 11382, Palo Alto CA 94306.

Womanshine. c/o Nancy Sundell, 6352 W 37th St, Indianapolis IN 46224. (317) 299-6336.

Womansong Theatre.   P.O. Box 15462, Atlanta GA 30333.

Womanspace Theatre.   c/o Carol Grosberg, 164 E 7th St,
     apt 4-R, New York NY 10009.   (212) 475-5261.

Women's Coffee Coven.   Seattle's Feminist Entertainment
     Center, P.O. Box 5104, Seattle WA 98105.

Women's Ensemble.   c/o Rebecca Goldstein, 2431 Echo Park
     Ave, Los Angeles CA 90026.

Women's Experimental Theatre.   98 E 7th St, New York   NY
     10009.

Women's Street Theatre.   People's Press, 968 Valencia St,
     San Francisco CA 94110.

Women's Theatre Council.   Maria Irene Fornés, 1 Sheridan
     Square, New York NY 10014.   (212) 989-7216.

The Womyn's Theatre.   c/o Mary Schultz, 6757 Palatine
     Ave N, Seattle WA 98103.   (206) 782-0657.

The World Woman's Culture Caravan.   P.O. Box 3488,
     Ridgeway Sta, Stamford CT 06905.

INDEX